BIRNBAUM GUIDES

W9-BOL-776

2014

Disney Cruise Line

Wendy Lefkon **EDITORIAL DIRECTOR**

Jill Safro **EDITOR**

Jessica Ward **CONTRIBUTING EDITOR**

Pam Brandon **CONTRIBUTING WRITER**

Clark Wakabayashi **DESIGNER**

Alexandra Mayes Birnbaum **CONSULTING EDITOR**

THE **OFFICIAL** GUIDE

DISNEY EDITIONS

NEW YORK • LOS ANGELES

For Steve Birnbaum, who merely made all this possible.

Other 2014 Birnbaum's Official Disney Guides:
Disneyland
Walt Disney World
Walt Disney World Dining
Walt Disney World For Kids
Walt Disney World Pocket Parks Guide

SUSTAINABLE
FORESTRY
INITIATIVE
Certified Chain of Custody
Promoting Sustainable Forestry
www.sfiprogram.org
SFI-00993

A WORD FROM THE EDITOR

Birnbaum editors are notoriously proud of their knowledge when it comes to all things Disney. After all, we've been gathering expertise about Disney theme parks for more decades than we care to admit. But luxury ocean liners? Tropical islands? Foreign ports of call? These represented some seriously uncharted waters for us . . . until we created this, our annually updated official guide to Disney Cruise Line. After comprehensive, grueling (yeah, right) research, we happily boast expert status in this area, and we're eager to share what we have learned.

For starters, we quickly realized that a voyage with the Mouse is atypical in a number of ways. Most obviously, there's the simultaneous (and successful) catering to families with kids and grown-ups *sans* offspring. In fact, each ship has programming designed to draw young, old, and those in between to entirely different recreational areas. Then there's the innovative "rotational dining system," a lineup of lavish musical productions, deck-shaking dance parties with Disney characters, and, of course, the possibility of a unique grand finale: a full day at Castaway Cay—a private, almost-too-good-to-be-true tropical island.

Like swaying in a hammock in the aforementioned paradise, the idea of purchasing a vacation package may lull one into an "everything is taken care of" sense of security. The truth is, there are still dozens of decisions to make, staterooms to select, shore excursions to book, etc. Within these pages, as with any Birnbaum guide, you'll find detailed, accurate information meant to help you plan a successful vacation.

Of course, even with our rigorous research missions (which, incidentally, began with the inaugural sailing of the *Disney Magic* in the summer of 1998), this book would not exist without the contributions of so many. To begin with, we owe a big thank-you to the folks at Disney Cruise Line. Although all editorial decisions are made by the Birnbaum staff, it's Disney Cruise Line's willingness to explain operations and provide factual data that makes this the Official Guide.

I'd like to extend a boatload of gratitude to Jonathan Frontado, Jara Church, Noel Myerson, Marcy Storm, Larry Stauffer, Shelley Gold Witiak, Maureen Landry, and Jennifer Haile-Tinn for the care and effort that they have put into this project.

For their key roles behind the scenes, we salute Jerry Gonzalez, Jennifer Eastwood, Diane Hodges, Michelle Olveira, Tracey Randinelli, Heather Pommerencke, Stacey Cook, Joan Peterson, and Mike Carroll.

Of course, no list of acknowledgments is complete without our founding editor, Steve Birnbaum, as well as Alexandra Mayes Birnbaum, who continues to provide gentle guidance and invaluable insight.

Finally, it's important to remember that specifics do change. To that end, we refine and expand our material with each annual revision. For the present edition, though, this is the final word.

Bon Voyage!

Jill Safro
—Editor

WHAT DO YOU THINK?

Nothing is more valuable to us than your comments on what we've written and on your own experiences with Disney Cruise Line. Please share your insights with us by writing to:

Birnbaum's Official Guide to Disney Cruise Line 2014
Disney Editions
1133 Sixth Avenue, 33rd Floor
New York, NY 10036
Attn: Jill Safro

TABLE OF CONTENTS

BEFORE YOU SAIL

Planning Ahead

The fact that you are holding this book means that you have probably decided to make Disney your cruise vacation choice. Now comes the hard part: Which cruise package is best for you? How do you book it? What should you do to prepare for the voyage? The chapter that follows should answer these questions and help—whether this is your first cruise or your 50th—make the idea of a Disney cruise a reality.

Selecting a Cruise

What to do, what to do. There are many factors to consider when choosing a cruise package. Among the most important are destination, budget, time available, stateroom needs, and preferred itinerary.

If you want to take the most inexpensive cruise possible, then a shorter cruise in a standard inside stateroom is probably a good choice. If money is no object, consider a 7-night adventure in the super-deluxe Walt Disney Suite. Of course, there are plenty of things in between—including pairing a Disney Cruise with a stay at Walt Disney World (see page 218). As for itineraries, there is a multitude of options from which to choose. What follows is a rundown of the itineraries that were most widely offered at press time.

SELECT ITINERARIES*

4-Night Bahamian Cruise—DISNEY DREAM
Itinerary A

DAY	ITINERARY
Day 1	Check in at Port Canaveral Terminal. Aboard by 3:45 P.M.
Day 2	Ashore at Nassau at 9:30 A.M. Aboard by 5:45 P.M.
Day 3	Ashore at Castaway Cay at 8:30 A.M. Aboard by 4:30 P.M.
Day 4	Full day at sea.
Day 5	Ship at Port Canaveral beginning at 7:30 A.M.

3-Night Bahamian Cruise—DISNEY DREAM
Itinerary A

DAY	ITINERARY
Day 1	Check in at Port Canaveral Terminal. Aboard by 3:45 P.M.
Day 2	Ashore at Nassau at 9:30 A.M. Aboard by 5:45 P.M.
Day 3	Ashore at Castaway Cay at 8:30 A.M. Aboard by 4:30 P.M.
Day 4	Ship at Port Canaveral beginning at 7:30 A.M.

4-Night Bahamian Cruise—DISNEY MAGIC
Itinerary B

DAY	ITINERARY
Day 1	Check in at Port Canaveral Terminal. Aboard by 4 P.M.
Day 2	Ashore at Nassau at 9:30 A.M. Aboard by 5:45 P.M.
Day 3	Ashore at Castaway Cay at 8:30 A.M. Aboard by 4:45 P.M.
Day 4	Full day at sea.
Day 5	Ship at Port Canaveral Terminal beginning at 7:30 A.M.

4-Night Bahamian Cruise—DISNEY WONDER
Itinerary B

DAY	ITINERARY
Day 1	Check in at Miami Terminal. Aboard by 4 P.M.
Day 2	Ashore at Castaway Cay at 8:30 A.M. Aboard by 4:45 P.M.
Day 3	Ashore at Nassau at 7 A.M. Aboard by 3:45 P.M.
Day 4	Ashore at Key West at 12 P.M. Aboard by 5:45 P.M.
Day 5	Ship at Miami Terminal beginning at 7:30 A.M.

* Itineraries and times were correct at press time but are subject to change for 2014. For additional itinerary options, visit *www.disneycruise.com.*

5-Night Western Caribbean Cruise—DISNEY WONDER
Itinerary A

DAY	ITINERARY
Day 1	Check in at Miami Terminal. Aboard by 4 P.M.
Day 2	Full day at sea.
Day 3	Ashore at Cozumel, Mexico, at 8:30 A.M. Aboard by 5:30 P.M.
Day 4	Full day at sea.
Day 5	Ashore at Castaway Cay at 8:30 A.M. Aboard by 4:30 P.M.
Day 6	Ship at Miami Terminal beginning at 7:30 A.M.

5-Night Western Caribbean Cruise—DISNEY WONDER
Itinerary B

DAY	ITINERARY
Day 1	Check in at Miami Terminal. Aboard by 4 P.M.
Day 2	Full day at sea.
Day 3	Ashore at Grand Cayman,* Cayman Islands, at 7:45 A.M. Aboard by 3:30 P.M.
Day 4	Ashore at Cozumel, Mexico, at 10:45 A.M. Aboard by 5:30 P.M.
Day 5	Full day at sea.
Day 6	Ship at Miami Terminal beginning at 7:30 A.M.

* Tendering is required in Grand Cayman. (See page 80 for tendering details.)

7-Night Eastern Caribbean Cruise—DISNEY FANTASY
Itinerary A

DAY	ITINERARY
Day 1	Check in at Port Canaveral Terminal. Aboard by 3:45 P.M.
Day 2	Full day at sea.
Day 3	Full day at sea.
Day 4	Ashore at St. Maarten at 8 A.M. Aboard by 6:45 P.M.
Day 5	Ashore at St. Thomas* at 7:45 A.M. (It's possible to experience excursions to St. John, too.) Aboard by 3:30 P.M.
Day 6	Full day at sea.
Day 7	Ashore at Castaway Cay at 9:45 A.M. Aboard by 4:45 P.M.
Day 8	Ship at Port Canaveral beginning at 7:30 A.M.

* Tendering is required in St. Thomas for select sail dates.

7-Night Eastern Caribbean Cruise—DISNEY FANTASY
Itinerary B

DAY	ITINERARY
Day 1	Check in at Port Canaveral Terminal. Aboard by 3:45 P.M.
Day 2	Full day at sea.
Day 3	Full day at sea.
Day 4	Ashore at St. Thomas* at 8 A.M. (It's possible to experience excursions to St. John, too.) Aboard by 5:30 P.M.
Day 5	Ashore at San Juan, Puerto Rico, at 7:45 A.M. Aboard by 4:45 P.M.
Day 6	Full day at sea.
Day 7	Ashore at Castaway Cay at 9:45 A.M. Aboard by 4:30 P.M.
Day 8	Ship at Port Canaveral beginning at 7:30 A.M.

* Tendering is required in St. Thomas for select sail dates.

5-Night Western Caribbean Cruise—DISNEY MAGIC
Itinerary A

DAY	ITINERARY
Day 1	Check in at Miami Terminal. Aboard by 4 P.M.
Day 2	Full day at sea.
Day 3	Ashore at Cozumel, Mexico, at 8:30 A.M. Aboard at 5:30 P.M.
Day 4	Full day at sea.
Day 5	Ashore at Castaway Cay at 8:30 A.M. Aboard by 4:30 P.M.
Day 6	Ship at Miami Terminal beginning at 7:30 A.M.

5-Night Western Caribbean Cruise—DISNEY MAGIC
Itinerary B

DAY	ITINERARY
Day 1	Check in at Miami Terminal. Aboard by 4 P.M.
Day 2	Full day at sea.
Day 3	Ashore at Grand Cayman*, Cayman Islands, at 7:45 A.M. Aboard by 3:30 P.M. (tendering required)
Day 4	Ashore at Cozumel, Mexico, at 10:45 A.M. Aboard by 5:30 P.M.
Day 5	Full day at sea.
Day 6	Ship at Miami Terminal beginning at 7:30 A.M.

* Tendering is required in Grand Cayman.

7-Night Eastern Caribbean Cruise—DISNEY FANTASY
Itinerary C

DAY	ITINERARY
Day 1	Check in at Port Canaveral Terminal. Aboard by 3:45 P.M.
Day 2	Full day at sea.
Day 3	Full day at sea.
Day 4	Ashore at St. Maarten at 8 A.M. Aboard by 6:45 P.M.
Day 5	Ashore at San Juan, Puerto Rico, at 7:45 A.M. Aboard by 4:45 P.M.
Day 6	Full day at sea.
Day 7	Ashore at Castaway Cay at 9:30 A.M. Aboard by 4:45 P.M.
Day 8	Ship at Port Canaveral beginning at 7:30 A.M.

7-Night Western Caribbean Cruise—DISNEY FANTASY
Itinerary B

DAY	ITINERARY
Day 1	Check in at Port Canaveral Terminal. Aboard by 3:45 P.M.
Day 2	Full day at sea.
Day 3	Ashore at Grand Cayman, Cayman Islands, at 11:30 A.M. Aboard by 4:45 P.M. (tendering required)
Day 4	Ashore at Costa Maya, Mexico, at 1 P.M. Aboard by 5:30 P.M.
Day 5	Ashore at Cozumel, Mexico, at 8:30 A.M. Aboard by 5:30 P.M.
Day 6	Full day at sea.
Day 7	Ashore at Castaway Cay at 9:30 A.M. Aboard by 4:30 P.M.
Day 8	Ship at Port Canaveral beginning at 7:30 A.M.

7-Night Southern Caribbean Cruise—DISNEY MAGIC
Itinerary A*

DAY	ITINERARY
Day 1	Check in at San Juan, Puerto Rico, Terminal. Aboard by 7 P.M.
Day 2	Full day at sea.
Day 3	Ashore at St. John's, Antigua, at 7 A.M. Aboard by 4:45 P.M.
Day 4	Ashore at Castries, St. Lucia, at 7:15 A.M. Aboard by 4:45 P.M.
Day 5	Ashore at St. George's, Grenada, at 7 A.M. Aboard at 4:45 P.M.
Day 6	Ashore at Bridgetown, Barbados, at 7 A.M. Aboard at 4:45 P.M.
Day 7	Ashore at Basseterre, St. Kitts, at 12 P.M. Aboard at 5:30 P.M.
Day 8	Ship at San Juan, Puerto Rico, Terminal beginning at 7 A.M.

* At press time, this itinerary was available on a limited basis. For details on the ports of call and excursions for this itinerary, visit *www.disneycruise.com*.

7-Night Alaska Cruise—DISNEY WONDER
Itinerary A

DAY	ITINERARY
Day 1	Check in at Vancouver Terminal. Aboard by 4 P.M.
Day 2	Full day at sea.
Day 3	Full day at sea (Tracy Arm, Alaska).
Day 4	Ashore at Skagway, Alaska, at 7:15 A.M. Aboard by 7:30 P.M.
Day 5	Ashore at Juneau, Alaska, at 6:15 A.M. Aboard by 4:30 P.M.
Day 6	Ashore at Ketchikan, Alaska, at 12:15 P.M. Aboard by 7:30 P.M.
Day 7	Full day at sea.
Day 8	Ship at Vancouver Terminal beginning at 8:00 A.M.

7-Night Western Caribbean Cruise—DISNEY WONDER
Itinerary A

DAY	ITINERARY
Day 1	Check in at Galveston Terminal. Aboard by 3:30 P.M.
Day 2	Full day at sea.
Day 3	Full day at sea.
Day 4	Ashore at Falmouth, Jamaica, at 7:45 A.M. Aboard at 5:45 P.M.
Day 5	Ashore at Grand Cayman, Cayman Islands, at 7:30 A.M. Aboard by 3:30 P.M. (tendering required)
Day 6	Ashore at Cozumel, Mexico, at 10:15 A.M. Aboard at 3:45 P.M.
Day 7	Full day at sea.
Day 8	Ship at Galveston Terminal beginning at 8:30 A.M.

7-Night Western Caribbean Cruise—DISNEY FANTASY
Itinerary C

DAY	ITINERARY
Day 1	Check in at Port Canaveral. Aboard by 3:45 P.M.
Day 2	Full day at sea.
Day 3	Ashore at Cozumel, Mexico, at 8:30 A.M. Aboard by 3:45 P.M.
Day 4	Ashore at Grand Cayman, Cayman Islands, at 10:30 A.M. Aboard by 5:30 P.M. (tendering is required)
Day 5	Ashore at Falmouth, Jamaica, at 7:30 A.M. Aboard by 4:45 P.M.
Day 6	Full day at sea.
Day 7	Ashore at Castaway Cay, at 8:30 A.M. Aboard at 4:45 P.M.
Day 8	Ship at Port Canaveral beginning at 7:30 A.M.

4-Night Vancouver to San Diego—DISNEY WONDER

DAY	ITINERARY
Day 1	Check in at Vancouver, Canada, Terminal. Aboard by 4 P.M.
Day 2	Ashore at Victoria, Canada, at 8:15 A.M. Aboard by 2:45 P.M.
Day 3	Full day at sea.
Day 4	Full day at sea.
Day 5	Ship at San Diego Terminal, beginning at 7:30 A.M.

7-Night Mediterranean Cruise—DISNEY MAGIC

DAY	ITINERARY
Day 1	Check in at Barcelona, Spain, Terminal. Aboard by 4 P.M.
Day 2	Full day at sea.
Day 3	Ashore at Villefranche, France,* at 7:45 A.M. Aboard by 6:30 P.M.
Day 4	Ashore at La Spezia, Italy,* at 7:45 A.M. Aboard by 7:30 P.M.
Day 5	Ashore at Civitavecchia, Italy, at 7:30 A.M. Aboard by 6:30 P.M.
Day 6	Ashore at Naples, Italy, at 7:30 A.M. Aboard by 5:30 P.M.
Day 7	Full day at sea.
Day 8	Ship at Barcelona Terminal beginning at 7 A.M.

* Tendering is required.

4-Night Mediterranean Cruise—DISNEY MAGIC

DAY	ITINERARY
Day 1	Check in at Barcelona, Spain, Terminal. Aboard by 4 P.M.
Day 2	Ashore at Villefranche, France,* at 8:45 A.M. Aboard by 6:30 P.M.
Day 3	Full day at sea.
Day 4	Ashore at Palma, Mallorca (Spain), at 7:45 A.M. Aboard by 6 P.M.
Day 5	Ship at Barcelona Terminal beginning at 7 A.M.

* Tendering is required in Villefranche.

12-Night Mediterranean Cruise—DISNEY MAGIC

DAY	ITINERARY
Day 1	Check in at Barcelona, Spain, Terminal. Aboard by 4 P.M.
Day 2	Ashore at Villefranche, France,* at 8:45 A.M. Aboard by 6:30 P.M.
Day 3	Ashore at La Spezia, Italy,* at 7:45 A.M. Aboard by 7:30 P.M.
Day 4	Ashore at Civitavecchia, Italy, at 7:15 A.M. Aboard by 6:30 P.M.
Day 5	Full day at sea.
Day 6	Full day at sea.
Day 7	Ashore at Piraeus, Greece, at 8 A.M. Ashore by 6:30 P.M.
Day 8	Ashore at Kusadasi, Turkey, at 7:30 A.M. Aboard by 6:30 P.M.
Day 9	Ashore at Mykonos, Greece, at 7:30 A.M. Aboard by 6:30 P.M.
Day 10	Full day at sea.
Day 11	Ashore at Valletta, Malta, at 7:45 A.M. Aboard by 5 P.M.
Day 12	Full day at sea.
Day 13	Ship at Barcelona Terminal beginning at 7 A.M.

* Tendering is required in La Spezia and Villefranche.

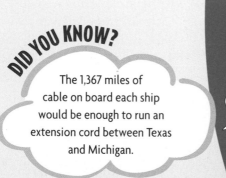

DID YOU KNOW?

The 1,367 miles of cable on board each ship would be enough to run an extension cord between Texas and Michigan.

Check Your Calendar

Determining the length of your cruise depends on several things—the first, how much time do you have in your busy schedule to devote to leisure? If your answer is only four days, don't despair: Disney has short cruises to the Bahamas (most of which include a stop at Disney's own private island, Castaway Cay). If you have at least a week, you may choose a 7-night-or-longer cruise to Alaska, the Caribbean, or the Mediterranean. For details, call 800-910-3659 or visit *www.disneycruise.com*.

Check Your Checkbook

The cost of your cruise is the next issue on the planning board. Budget constraints can be eased in several ways: by taking one of the shorter cruises, choosing a less expensive stateroom class, and by limiting the number of land tours and excursions you take at the various ports of call. (We often forgo pricey excursions because the ships themselves have so much to offer.) Plan to eat aboard the ship, too—meals and snacks are included in the vacation package, as are many extras, including stage shows, movies, tours, lectures, games, bands, deck parties with characters, and more.

WWW.DISNEYCRUISE.COM

We've done our best to provide accurate, current information regarding all things Disney Cruise Line. That said, rates, itineraries, excursions, and other specifics are subject to change. For additional information or to book a cruise, excursion, and more, visit the interactive website: *www. disneycruise.com*. The site is one of the most user-friendly websites we have ever seen.

WHAT'S NOT INCLUDED

Rest assured that all of your basic vacation needs are covered by the "all-inclusive" price of the cruise. However, there are always "extras" that you may want to ante up a little cash for. Here's a list of items and services that carry an extra charge:

- ⚓ Child care for ages 3 and under (see pages 43 and 115)
- ⚓ Port Adventures (aka shore excursions)
- ⚓ Expenses incurred while on land in ports of call (with the exception of food and most soft drinks at Castaway Cay)
- ⚓ Alcoholic beverages
- ⚓ Palo and Remy (These optional, reservations-necessary, adults-only restaurants carry an extra charge: about $20 per person for dinner and brunch at Palo; about $50 per person for champagne brunch and $75 for dinner at Remy.)
- ⚓ Refreshments at Cove Cafe, Vibe, and any bar or lounge
- ⚓ Spa treatments
- ⚓ Arcade games and sports simulators
- ⚓ Photographs snapped by the ship's photographers
- ⚓ Internet usage (see page 50)
- ⚓ Cell phone usage (see page 50)
- ⚓ Ship-to-shore telephone calls (There is a sizable fee for all calls, incoming and outgoing. Calls within the ship are free.)

With the exception of non-Disney ports of call, all "incidental" charges will be billed to your stateroom, provided that you leave a credit card imprint upon check-in. It's a good idea to have some cash on hand (we bring about $300, just in case), but there are few chances to use it. Except for tips, cash isn't accepted on the ships. Same goes for Castaway Cay, with the exception of the post office—stamps must be purchased with cash. Most of the non-Disney port shops accept major credit cards, and most accept U.S. currency.

GROUND TRANSFERS

Disney Cruise Line provides reliable, friendly service aboard its motor coaches (aka: buses). Getting to the buses is easy. Upon arrival at Orlando International Airport, take a shuttle to the Main Terminal. Once there, proceed to Disney's Magical Express Welcome Center. It's on Level One, Side B. The real bonus here is the baggage handling: For flights before 10 P.M., Disney reps will pull your tagged luggage and make sure it gets delivered to your room. (Guests arriving after 10 P.M. may collect their luggage and proceed to the Magical Express Welcome Center.) From the airport, a bus will take you to Port Canaveral or a WDW hotel. (For guests with transfers included in their cruise package, your bus departure location and information is included in your cruise documentation.) What if you're staying at a resort that's not designated as a departure location or at an off-property hotel? You'll have to get yourself to one of the WDW departure spots to catch a bus to the ship! Here's the pricing for Orlando ground transfers:

TRANSFER TRIP	PRICE*
Airport to select WDW resort (one-way)	Free**
Select WDW resort to Port Canaveral	$35
Round-trip from Orlando International Airport (MCO) to Port Canaveral	$70
Land and Sea vacation (Orlando airport to select WDW resort; WDW resort to Port Canaveral; Port Canaveral to airport)	$70

*Prices are per person, were correct at press time, and are subject to change.
**Disney's Magical Express transportation is a free service for WDW resort guests. For pricing details about transfers to and from other locations, call 800-951-3532.

Selecting a Stateroom

Sure, you'd like the largest suite on the ship. No question, you want the biggest verandah. And, of course, you absolutely must have a great view. But if that doesn't fit your budget, there are other appealing options. Consider this: Every stateroom boasts nautical decor, has ample closet space, a television, and a small safe. Inside staterooms can be a bit less expensive and not much smaller than their outside counterparts; on the *Dream* and the *Fantasy* they have virtual portholes (aka "magical" portholes, these high-tech wonders have HD digital screens). On the other hand, should you decide to splurge, know that there are concierge rooms and larger suites with private verandahs where you can savor a refreshing beverage and read the newest page-turner, periodically taking a moment to gaze at the sea.

Of course, there are other factors to think about when selecting a stateroom. How many people are in your party? Are you traveling with young children? Perhaps a Deluxe Stateroom would suit your family's needs. These accommodations have queen-size beds, bunk beds for the

WHAT'S IN A NAME?

A whole lot, when it comes to Disney Cruise Line accommodations. Here's a listing of the types of rooms available on each of the ships. Note that it is possible to request side-by-side staterooms, but it can't be guaranteed. For specifics on stateroom amenities, turn to page 74.

- ⚓ Standard Inside Stateroom
- ⚓ Deluxe Inside Stateroom
- ⚓ Deluxe Ocean-view Stateroom
- ⚓ Deluxe Family Ocean-view Stateroom (*Dream* and *Fantasy*)
- ⚓ Deluxe Ocean-view Stateroom with Navigator's Verandah
- ⚓ Deluxe Ocean-view Stateroom with Verandah
- ⚓ Deluxe Family Ocean-view Stateroom with Verandah
- ⚓ Concierge Family Ocean-view Stateroom with Verandah (*Dream* and *Fantasy*)
- ⚓ Concierge 1-Bedroom Suite with Verandah
- ⚓ Concierge 2-Bedroom Suite with Verandah (*Magic* and *Wonder*)
- ⚓ Concierge Royal Suite with Verandah

kids, and a split bath (see page 75). A curtained divider provides a bit of privacy.

Of course, there's always the Walt Disney Suite and the Roy E. Disney Suite—so if money is no object, treat your crew to one of these thousand-plus-square-foot homes away from home. No matter what your requirements are, chances are Disney Cruise Line can meet them.

How to Book a Cruise

In addition to using *www.disneycruise.com* or calling Disney Cruise Line (800-910-3659), many guests book through travel agents.

PAYMENT METHODS
Cruise packages, as well as incidentals, gratuities, hotel bills, and deposits, may be paid by credit card (Visa, MasterCard, JCB Card, American Express, Diners Club, Disney Visa, etc.), traveler's check, cashier's

check, money order, or personal check. Personal checks must bear the guest's name and address, be drawn on a U.S. bank, and be accompanied by proper identification (a valid driver's license with photo or government-issued photo ID). The reservation number should be written on the face of the check. Checks will not be accepted within 21 days prior to vacation commencement date. Keep in mind that the final

HOT TIP

Guests who plan to arrive at Port Canaveral the night before setting sail might consider staying at one of these resorts on nearby Astronaut Boulevard:
● Country Inns & Suites by Carlson. Rates range from $89–$129, and there is a shuttle to the cruise terminal; 321-784-8500 or 888-201-1746.
● Residence Inn by Marriott. Rates range from $169–$220; 321-323-1100 or 800-331-3131.

payment for a cruise package must be made *between 75 and 150 days* prior to the cruise, depending on the itinerary and category. Final payment due date varies for special itineraries.

Payments sent via mail should be addressed to:
Disney Cruise Line
P.O. Box 277763
Atlanta, GA 30384-7763

Payments sent via courier service (i.e., FedEx or UPS) should be sent to:
Disney Cruise Line
Bank of America
Lockbox Services
Lockbox 277763
6000 Feldwood Road
College Park, GA 30349
(407-566-3500)

DEPOSIT REQUIREMENTS
When you book a trip, you'll get a "due date" for a deposit. The deposit is 20 percent of the cruise fare. Reservations will be canceled if a deposit is not received by the deadline. (Packages that are booked within the final payment due date or in categories IGT, OGT, and VGT get special instructions.)

CANCELLATION POLICY
Though cancellations may be made by telephone or by mail, we suggest the phone.

Fees paid for canceling depend on when that call is made. For cruises of less than 10 days where embark or debark is a U.S. port, cancellation fees are as follows:
• For all suites and concierge rooms, cancellation within 74 to 45 days of sail date costs the deposit per guest.
• For each stateroom guest, canceling 74 to 45 before sailing costs the deposit.
• For all rooms, a cancellation within 44 to 30 days costs 50 percent of the vacation price.
• For all staterooms, a cancellation within 29 to 15 days costs 75 percent per guest.
• Should a cruise be canceled less than 14 days ahead, you'll

pay for the whole package.

For cruises 10 days or more and less than 10 days where embark and debark is a *non-U.S. port*, the fees are as follows:

• For all staterooms, canceling within 119 to 56 days or more before the sailing costs the deposit per guest.

• Canceling within 55 to 30 days costs 50 percent of the vacation cost per guest.

• Canceling within 29 to 15 days costs 75 percent of the vacation package per guest.

• Canceling less than 14 days ahead means you'll pay for the whole package.

To avoid the sad fate of paying for a canceled cruise, we recommend insuring your trip. For details, see page 36.

What to Pack

"Cruise Casual" is the operative phrase with Disney. Shorts, T-shirts, sundresses, and the like are fine daytime wear. At

IDENTIFICATION PAPERS

Unlike a visit to Walt Disney World's Epcot, where it only feels as if you're leaving the country, in the case of a Disney Cruise Line vacation, you really do. Given that, you'll need to provide proper proof of citizenship when passing through Customs. U.S. government regulations related to passport requirements are subject to change. Therefore, all guests should have a valid passport for all cruises. Call 877-487-2778 or visit *http://travel. state.gov* for current requirements.

HOT TIP

You will always have to show your "Key to the World" card (Disney-issued stateroom key and ID) when disembarking or boarding the ship. Adults also need a government-issued photo ID (a passport is ideal).

dinnertime, casual takes on a more formal meaning: Set aside the shorts and plan on slacks (jeans are okay, except at Palo and Remy) and a collared shirt for men, with real shoes, as opposed to those of the tennis variety. The same goes for women, while dresses are suitable, too. On 7-night-or-longer cruises, there is a semi-formal and a formal night. While some folks don black tie and sequins, it's not necessary to break out formal wear if you prefer a more casual look. On these occasions, the *Personal Navigator* (see page 81) will tip you off as to the appropriate attire. Many guests pack pirate garb, too, in anticipation of "Pirates IN the Caribbean" party night—don't forget to pack your puffy shirt and eye patch. (The Pirates IN the Caribbean party takes place on most sailings.)

Bathing suits are a must, as are beach shoes, wraps, sunscreen, sunglasses, and hats. Some sundries, such as shampoo, conditioner, and body lotion, are provided in your stateroom. Others are available for purchase, but the prices are steep, and the shops aren't always open (U.S. Customs limits the operating hours). Take an inventory of the products you'll need daily, and be sure to bring them. Here's a checklist of must-haves: passport, cash, memory card, chargers, waterproof ID holder, prescription medication (in original containers), at least one "dressy" outfit, and comfortable shoes.

Pack a Day Bag

Guests may check in at the port and board the ship as early as 1 P.M., but your checked luggage may not arrive until 6 P.M. (though usually earlier). Keep in mind that you will have access to your stateroom beginning at 1:30 P.M., along with most shipboard amenities, including all pools, so pack your swimsuit in a day bag. This should serve as, or fit in, a carry-on, as checked bags will be out of your hands once you surrender them. (Day bags can't be larger than 9 inches by 14 inches by 22 inches and do not count as part of the two-bag-per-passenger quota.) The bag should also include your passports, valuables, breakable items, and anything else you might need during those first hours on board. Note that most airlines require that carried-on liquids be in 3.4-ounce-or-smaller containers and fit into one quart-size, clear, plastic zip-top bag.

Booking Shore Excursions

All prospective Disney Cruise Line guests should know as much as possible about the tours and activities that are offered at each port of call, so it makes sense to visit *www.disneycruise.com* for updates. Our *Ports of Call* chapter offers descriptions of many of the most popular Caribbean, Alaskan, and Bahamian excursions (plus other destinations), along with a personal reaction. (Note that specifics about certain 2014 excursions itineraries were not available at press time.) Cancellations or changes may be made up to 3 days before the start of a cruise to receive a full refund. After that, you pay whether you play or not.

Port Adventures (also known as Shore Excursions) are quite popular and tend to fill up early. To book yours, visit *www.disneycruise. com*. To make last-minute arrangements, visit your ship's Port Adventures desk. Note that Port Adventures are not operated by the Walt Disney Company—not even those on Castaway Cay.

INSURE YOUR TRIP

Nobody books a vacation expecting to cancel it—yet sometimes life intervenes and it's unavoidable. That's why we strongly advise you to make travel insurance a part of your vacation budget. (We always do.) The Vacation Protection Plan provides baggage, trip cancellation/interruption, and medical-expense coverage for the duration of the cruise. The cost is calculated per guest and is eight percent of the cruise fare. All rates are subject to change. The Vacation Protection plan is not provided by the Walt Disney Company. Call 800-910-3659 for additional information. Here's an overview of what's covered:

⚓ Trip cancellation/interruption protection (for medical reasons or other specific issues)

⚓ Travel-delay protection (for additional travel expenses incurred by you due to covered travel delays)

⚓ Emergency medical/dental benefits for the duration of your cruise (includes transportation to the nearest appropriate medical facility). Medical expenses may need to be paid upfront and submitted for reimbursement once guests are home. Reimbursements are at the discretion of the insurance provider.

⚓ Baggage coverage (for lost or delayed arrival of baggage)

⚓ A 24-hour hotline to help with the replacement of lost travel documents or emergency cash transfers. (From the United States, call 877-593-4988; outside the U.S., call 804-281-5700. The program ID number is 001000287.)

How to Get to Port Canaveral

By Plane

Fly to Orlando International Airport. We prefer to arrive the night before or take a flight that is scheduled to arrive in the early morning hours. (That helps avoid potential travel delays.) If you get there on the early side, you can make a day of it. And, if your flight is delayed, you'll still have a shot at making it to the port before the ship sails. (When you book your cruise, ask about the check-in cutoff time. Don't be late!)

From the Airport

As you get off the shuttle and enter the main terminal, proceed directly to the Disney Magical Express Welcome Center. It's on Level 1, Side B of the terminal. After your party has checked in, a Disney rep will direct you toward a motor coach. Don't worry about checked luggage. For guests with transfers, all bags bearing appropriate tags will be claimed by Disney and delivered to your stateroom. (If you are driving to the ship, refer to page 39.)

ALL GOOD THINGS . . .

How time flies when you're having fun. You blink and it's time to go home! Here are a few tips about the debarkation process.

The day before your return to the debarkation terminal, you'll receive an information packet that includes a set of colored luggage tags. The color coding designates the area of the terminal in which you can pick them up. Be sure to remove the original tags from the inbound trip before you put new tags on all bags. (Guest Services has extra tags.) You'll also get a U.S. Customs form when applicable. Hand this form in as you leave the terminal.

On the night before debarkation, you'll place luggage outside your stateroom. (Bags will be collected and delivered to a color-coded area at the terminal.) Keep valuables, clothing for debarkation, medications, tickets, passports, and other key documents with you. (You have the option of "express walk off" if you're able to take your own bags off the ship in the morning.) Your waitstaff will tell you about last-morning breakfast options. After breakfast, it's time to leave the ship, taking all your happy memories and, quite possibly, the promise to return again soon. Of course, guests participating in onboard airline check-in don't have to claim bags until their plane lands at their home airport.

The following details apply to cruises departing from Port Canaveral, Florida. For details, call 800-910-3659 or visit *www. disneycruise.com.*

Disney Motor Coach
The bus trip from Orlando International Airport or a Disney World resort to Port Canaveral takes about 90 minutes (without traffic). While onboard, you can fill out paperwork (though it is best to do this ahead of time). There's a restroom on-board. Motor coach transportation may be purchased with a cruise package.

Car Service
Noris Limousine and Florida Towncar offer friendly, reliable service between Orlando International Airport (MCO) and Port Canaveral. For rates, information, or to make a reservation with Noris Limousine, call 407-

240-4533, or visit *www. norislimousine.com.* For Florida Towncar, go to *www. floridatowncar.com,* or call 800-525-7246 or 407-277-5466. Reservations are necessary, and cancellations must be made at least 48 hours in advance. Disney Cruise Line's reservations department can take your car service request, too.

Automobile
Disney Cruise Line's Port Canaveral Terminal is located on the north side or "A" Cruise Terminals; 9155 Charles M. Rowland Drive, Port Canaveral, Florida, 32920. It's about a 90-minute drive from Orlando International Airport and from Walt Disney World. The large parking facility, which is

TAG YOUR BAGS

Flying to Orlando International Airport for a cruise out of Port Canaveral? After you book your cruise and purchase ground transfers, you'll get a personalized info packet in the mail. Included in this valuable envelope will be colorful luggage tags. We cannot overemphasize the importance of affixing these tags to all checked luggage. Why? Once you say good-bye to your bags at the airport, you won't see them again until they arrive at your stateroom. Disney reps collect bags and deliver them to your stateroom by 6 P.M.

If you arrive by car or bus, drop your bags with porters at the terminal. They will be delivered to your stateroom for you.

If you'd rather not haul your bags off the ship, expect to use a similar color-coding method at the end of your cruise (this applies to all cruises). A set of tags will be left in your stateroom. Slap them on your bags, make a note of the color, and place them in the hall on the last night of the cruise. Look for them in the designated section of the terminal once you debark. *Guests participating in onboard airline check-in don't have to claim their bags until their plane lands at their home airport. Restrictions apply.*

COLD AND FLU ADVISORY

Disney Cruise Line follows extra-ordinary sanitation efforts to ensure the safety and comfort of guests. Even so, people can get sick. If you or a member of your party experience any symptom of illness (cold, flu, etc.) within 72 hours of sailing, you may be evaluated by a medical team. (If necessary, Cruise Line representatives will direct you to someone to help your party make alternate plans.)

Once on board, all guests are asked to wash their hands frequently and thoroughly—as this is a highly effective barrier to spreading germs. If you or someone in your party does become ill during your trip, head directly to the Medical Center. You'll be taken care of there, and immediate treatment will help limit the potential impact to others.

operated by the Canaveral Port Authority, accepts cash (U.S. currency), Visa, MasterCard, and traveler's checks *only*. Personal checks are not accepted. The cost to park is about $15 per day. Rates are subject to change.

From Orlando International Airport, take State Road (S.R.) 528 East (Beachline Expressway). Continue over the Indian River and the Banana River. Turn right onto S.R. 401, which will loop and head north over the channel locks. Stay in the right-hand lane and follow signs to the "A" Cruise Terminals. S.R. 528 is a toll road.

IMPORTANT NUMBERS

- Disney Cruise Line reservations and information: 800-910-3659
- Walt Disney World Central Reservations: 407-934-7639

If you are driving from Walt Disney World, take State Road 536 East to 417 (the GreeneWay). Follow 417 to S.R. 528 East (Beachline Expressway). At the fork in the road, veer right to stay on S.R. 528. Continue over the Indian and Banana rivers. Turn right onto S.R. 401. Stay in the right lane and follow signs leading to the "A" Cruise Terminals. Note that 417 and 528 are toll roads.

Guests who are driving from North Florida should take I-95 South exit #205 for S.R. 528 East (Beachline Expressway). Continue over the Indian and Banana rivers. Turn right onto S.R. 401. Stay in the right lane and follow signs to "A" Cruise Terminals.

Drivers originating in South Florida should take I-95 North. Exit at #205 for S.R. 528 East (The Beachline). Take S.R. 528 to S.R. 401. Keep to the right

HOT TIP

Disney Cruise Line has called Port Canaveral home since 1998 and will do so for the foreseeable future. For details on how to get to ports such as Galveston, Texas; Los Angeles, California; and more, visit *www.disneycruiseline.com*.

and follow the signs to "A" Cruise Terminals.

Getting to Port Canaveral from WDW (without a car)
Disney Cruise Line has buses to take guests directly from most WDW resorts, except the Swan and Dolphin. One-way transfers cost $35 per person, while $70 will cover the round-trip. Guests with transfers will get a letter in their resort room with departure details. Bell services will automatically pick up luggage when transfers have been pre-arranged. (Car services make the trip to and from Port Canaveral, too. See page 38 for details.)

LIGHTEN YOUR LUGGAGE

Traveling with an infant or toddler? Life just got easier for you! It's now possible to order baby supplies online and have them delivered directly to your stateroom. This Disney Cruise Line exclusive is provided by Babies Travel Lite and offers more than 1,000 brand-name products (diapers, baby food, formula, etc.). Access the service by visiting *www.disneycruise.com*.

Customized Travel Tips

Traveling with Babies

CRIBS

If you are traveling with a baby, it is possible to have a playpen-like, foldaway crib sent to your stateroom. (The cribs are 39.8 inches long, 28.25 inches wide, and 31.25 inches high.) Request one when you make a reservation, and confirm it before leaving home. (If you booked your cruise package through a travel agent, call said agent with requests such as this.) Supplies are limited. Bring a blanket, as the cribs come with fitted sheets only.

DIAPER SERVICE

It is possible to have a disposable diaper system sent to your stateroom. You can request it when you make a reservation, or speak with your Stateroom Host or Hostess upon arrival.

FOOD

Staterooms on the *Magic* and *Wonder* have a small "beverage cooler," which maintains a temperature of approximately 55 degrees.

Formula and food can be stored safely within the unit. (*Dream* and *Fantasy* staterooms have small refrigerators.) At least one shop on board sells diapers, formula, and a limited selection of food. (The shop isn't always open, as U.S. Customs limits its hours.) If you'd like to save money, pack as many baby rations as possible. Round-the-clock room service means you will never get caught with a screaming, hungry little one and no means of quelling the hunger pangs. Note that homemade baby food is not allowed on board.

BABYSITTING

Onboard babysitting is available for tots ages 12 weeks to 3 years. The cost is $6 an hour for the first child, with a one-hour minimum. Each additional child (who must be the first child's sibling) is $5 per hour. The service is offered in the ship's

MEDICINE STORAGE

All staterooms on the *Dream* and *Fantasy* have a mini fridge (perfectly suitable for storing medicine), but staterooms on the *Magic* and *Wonder* have a "beverage cooler." They are fine for storing food, but not necessarily medication (especially if it requires a stable temperature). Guests who need to store medicine should visit the ship's medical center or Guest Services, or request a small refrigerator. Availability is limited, so ask for one at the same time you reserve your cruise package. Call to confirm it before you leave.

HOT TIP

If you will be using an ECV (Electronic Conveyance Vehicle) during your cruise, be sure to book an accessible stateroom (other rooms can't accommodate ECVs). And note that no ECV parking is allowed in stateroom corridors or on elevator landings.

GETTING AROUND IT

Disabled travelers already know that travel requires a lot of advance planning. Disney has equipped its ships with a variety of amenities geared toward those guests with special needs.

Wheelchair-accessible state-rooms are equipped with ramp entrances to bathrooms, fold-down shower seats, handheld shower heads, lowered towel and closet racks, a bathroom phone, and emergency call buttons.

There is a limited number of sand wheelchairs available on Castaway Cay (first come, first served). *Note:* If you will need a wheelchair throughout the cruise, you are encouraged to bring your own.

Throughout the ship, there are wheelchair-accessible restrooms. Accessible pool lifts are available on the *Dream* and *Fantasy*.

Guests with hearing disabilities need not miss any of the fun on board. In-cabin TVs can be equipped with open-captioning, and assisted-listening devices are available at all theaters and show rooms. Also available are communication kits equipped with alarm clock, door-knock and telephone alerts with bed shaker notification. Make your needs known when you book your cruise.

nursery. Reservations can be made at *www.disneycruise. com* or on board (based on availability). In-room babysitting is not offered on any ship.

OTHER SUPPLIES

Diapers, pacifiers, pool toys, and more can be purchased on board. The ships' shops aren't always open, so take inventory and plan ahead to avoid being caught short. If it's an emergency, inquire at Guest Services. They can help with just about any onboard crisis.

Bottle sterilizers and bottle warmers are also available at the Guest Services desk. You can also order supplies in advance through Babies Travel Lite (see Lighten Your Luggage on page 42 for details).

Travelers with Disabilities

Measures have been taken to make your stay as comfortable and effortless

as possible. Disney Cruise Line offers special equipment and facilities for guests with disabilitics. Each ship has staterooms that are equipped for guests using wheelchairs. They have ramped bathroom thresholds, open bed frames, bathroom and shower handrails, fold-down shower seats, handheld showerheads, and lowered towel and closet bars. Open-captioning is available for stateroom televisions and for some onboard video monitors.

Stateroom communication kits may be reserved upon request. They include door-knock and phone alerts, phone amplifier, bed shaker notification, a strobe light smoke detector, and a text typewriter (aka TTY). There is no charge for the kit, but supplies are limited. Make your needs known when you make your reservation and confirm it prior to sailing. Wheelchair-accessible rest-rooms are available in several common areas on board. There are accessible pool lifts

45

on the *Dream* and *Fantasy*. A small number of sand wheelchairs are available on Castaway Cay. American Sign Language interpretation is available for live performances on various cruise dates. (The service is not available on every cruise, so be sure to start planning your trip as far in advance as possible.) For additional information or to make special requests, ask your reservationist. For more information via TTY (text typewriter), please call 407-566-7455.

If you have any questions or concerns once on board, pay a visit to the ship's Guest Services desk.

Travelers Without Children

This being a Disney cruise, one could argue that you—the footloose, fancy-free folks—are on their turf. And, as such, you might expect to have youngsters underfoot at all times. This is simply not the case. The Disney ships were designed with three specific types of vacationers in mind: families, kids, and grown-ups without kids. On board, there is an adults-only deck area, complete with its own pool (not to mention music and games). There's a gourmet restaurant (two on the *Dream* and *Fantasy*) and a cozy coffee bar. It goes without saying that those spots, as well as several lounges, are strictly for the grown-up set (as in adults with legal proof of age). Plus, there are countless other ways to enjoy a grown-up getaway in the various ports of call. With that in mind, Castaway Cay (Disney's private island) guarantees you and your ilk a piece of prime beachfront real estate where you can bask in the sun or read a novel in the shade without the fear of sand being kicked in your face. You can even have a massage in a cabana overlooking the ocean. Can you manage to spend days on end without encountering the wee ones of our species? No way. But who'd want to?

Medical Matters

The Medical Center, located forward on Deck 1, is open daily to assist with any medical emergencies or health concerns. Regular hours are from 9:30 A.M. to 11 A.M. and from 4:30 P.M. to 7 P.M. All Disney ships have a physician and nurse on call 24 hours a day (even while in port) for conditions that require immediate attention. Health services are provided by a company independent from Disney Cruise Line, and standard prevailing fees will be charged for all

IT'S NOT EASY BEING GREEN

Unfortunately, Mother Nature being predictably unpredictable, the seas are occasionally a tad turbulent. So, there's always the possibility that you or a member of your party may become a little green about the gills. Plan ahead. We recommend packing a supply of over-the-counter medication (but know these may make you drowsy). We also suggest you pack ginger pills (available at most health food and vitamin stores) and drink ginger ale.

If you've experienced motion sickness in the past, try to steer clear of inside cabins (though the virtual portholes on the *Dream* and *Fantasy* may help). Outer cabins have windows—and the view of the horizon can be a helpful stabilizer. If the room has a verandah, all the better. Fresh air may not be an antidote to nausea, but it can't hurt. Some find relief in the form of bitters mixed with water or club soda. Then there are sea bands. They fit snugly around the wrist, supposedly alleviating symptoms by hitting key pressure points. You can pick them up at many pharmacies.

The good news is, most people get their "sea legs" very quickly, adjusting to the motion (slight or otherwise) soon after setting sail.

services. Fees will be charged to your stateroom account.

In extreme cases, Disney Cruise Line will arrange to have a passenger taken to the nearest port to receive medical care.

The cost of this varies with the location of the ship and the nearest port. Because all health care provided qualifies as "care outside the United States," you will be responsible for paying any charges incurred while on board prior to debarkation and submitting the request for coverage to your insurance carrier (all paperwork will be provided).

If you get sick while on shore, your guide should direct you back to your ship's tour director at the dock, who will help you get back to the ship.

If you are diabetic and using insulin or take other medication that needs to be refrigerated during your cruise, you can arrange for

a small refrigerator to be brought to your cabin. Make your needs known well in advance. Pack a sufficient supply of prescription medications that you require and keep them with you at all times while traveling— including embarking and debarking the ship. (Always travel with medicines in their original containers.)

Regarding younger passengers, know that any child exhibiting symptoms of illness will not be allowed to participate in the youth activities or be cared for in the ship's nursery. Absolutely no exceptions.

Special Occasions

For many travelers, taking a cruise is a special occasion in and of itself. Still, lots of folks choose to celebrate birthdays, anniversaries, and other special events on board. If you fall into this category, be sure to tell your travel agent, call 800-910-3659, or visit *www.disneycruise.com* at least three weeks before you sail. There you can order a special wine, floral arrangement, specialty cake, or a gift package to celebrate any occasion. Some events, such as weddings and reunions, require a bit more planning.

Weddings

Whether you are saying your "I do's" for the first time, committing yourselves to each other, or renewing your vows, Disney Cruise Line has the means to make the occasion exceptionally memorable. Ceremonies may be performed on the ship or at Castaway Cay. Some happy couples invite family members along for the trip, while others prefer to have this time to themselves. For more information, call 321-939-4610, or contact your travel agent. Call as far in advance as possible and before you book your cruise.

HOT TIP

If you were hoping to treat Fido to a high-seas adventure, think again. With the exception of service animals, Disney Cruise Line enforces a strict "humans only" policy. You will not be permitted to board with a pet of any kind.

HOW TO CALL THE SHIP

Disney Cruise Line guests may be contacted by calling 888-322-8732 from the U.S. The international number is 1-732-335-3281. Rates range from about $7 to $9.50 per minute. Callers should have the name of the ship and the party they are calling. To specify the ship, they would select 1 for the *Dream*, 2 for the *Fantasy*, 3 for the *Magic*, and 4 for the *Wonder*. Payment may be made by credit card. Messages can be recorded via voice mail. Each call is limited to 10 minutes.

Some guests may also be reached by personal cell phone. Wireless service, available in staterooms only, is available to subscribers of a host of cellular providers worldwide. Rates vary.

HOT TIP

If you plan to use your cell phone during your cruise, be sure to check with your wireless provider before leaving home. Ask if you'll get service through them while on board and how much voice, data, and text service costs.

Fingertip Reference Guide

Business Services
Wait a minute, aren't you here to relax? For those of you who must get a little work done while at sea, there are some business services available for an additional charge. Among them are fax transmission, copies, and AV equipment. Wireless Internet service is available throughout the ships (including staterooms) for a fee. Guests access the Web via cell phone and various personal computing devices. There are several laptops with Internet access (for a fee) at the Cove Cafe on each ship. Note that the Wi-Fi service at sea can best be described as "low speed." Very low. Expect *lots* of buffering time and dropped connections. All staterooms have phones (ship-to-shore rates apply), and electrical outlets are laptop friendly. Note that the ships' computers don't accept uploads and do not

run any Microsoft Office applications (so any attachments from associated e-mail accounts cannot be opened). There is, however, a handy printer at the ready. Are you planning on holding meetings during your cruise? For details on business services, visit *www.disneymeetings.com*.

Camera Needs

By all means, bring a camera. Film and memory cards are sold on board. There are also many roving Disney photographers on the ship capturing moments throughout the day. You'll find shots taken at "static locations" (i.e., character sets in the lobby) are available

for viewing at photo kiosks at Shutters (the photo store on all Disney ships) and by the Promenade Lounge on the *Magic* and *Wonder*. Unlike the PhotoPass system at Walt Disney World, these photos may only be viewed and purchased during the cruise. All pictures taken by roaming photographers (i.e., in the dining rooms, by the pool, on Castaway Cay, etc.) may be viewed, printed, and purchased at Shutters on all four ships. Photos can be purchased on a single CD—one-stop shopping! The photos are very high in quality (and in price).

Drinking Laws

The drinking age on the ships is 21 and is strictly enforced. Valid government-issued photo ID is required. Disney Cruise Line reserves the right to refuse alcohol sales to anyone. On cruises departing from European countries where the legal

SHIPBOARD AMENITIES

Here's a rundown of some of the less obvious amenities provided by Disney Cruise Line. (Note that charges apply.)

⚓ Complete laundry, dry cleaning, and valet services

⚓ Photo center that processes photos in an hour and has camera and video recorder rentals

⚓ Self-service launderettes

⚓ Satellite phone service

⚓ Internet cafe (*Magic* and *Wonder* only)

⚓ Wireless Internet service (available in many public spaces. BYO laptop.)

⚓ Modern medical facilities with a doctor and nurse on call

⚓ Stroller rentals

⚓ Telefax and secretarial services (on request)

⚓ Conference facilities for groups of up to 120 (*Dream* only)

age is lower than 21, a legal guardian who is sailing with a passenger between the ages of 18 and 20 may sign a waiver allowing their charge to imbibe.

Mail

Letters and postcards may be mailed from the post office at Castaway Cay. Stamps are the only things available for purchase here (cash only). It is also possible to mail items from other ports—it's just less convenient. If you plan to buy stamps from the Castaway Cay post office, do so early. The office is operated by Bahamian authorities and may not be open late in the day. Even if it's closed for the day, you can still mail letters from the post office, and all items will be delivered with a Castaway Cay postmark. Note that postcards and stamps may be purchased on the ship.

Money Matters

There is no need for cash on the ship. You can apply a credit card to your account during the check-in process. (Most major credit cards, including MasterCard, JCB, Visa, and American Express, are accepted.) From then on, all you'll need to do is sign for extras you want (including excursions booked on the ship), and these amounts will be charged to that card.

Cash or credit cards will be necessary for meals, taxis, and other purchases made in all ports but Castaway Cay (where a stateroom key is accepted in all cases except for stamps, which must be bought with cash). A few hundred dollars should suffice. Standard gratuities are automatically prepaid and charged to your cruise folio. Extra gratuities may be charged to a stateroom or paid in cash. Special envelopes will be delivered

MONEY IN MEXICO

While major credit cards are accepted throughout most of Mexico, there are a few rules about using U.S. cash that travelers should know about:

● There is a limit on how much cash may be exchanged into pesos at hotels, exchange booths, and local banks. At press time, that limit was $1,500 per person, per month.

● Businesses (including restaurants, shops, and tour and travel companies) are permitted to accept a maximum of $100 (U.S. dollars) cash per transaction. (There are no restrictions on the number of transactions an individual can make.) For example, if an American traveler wants to purchase a snorkeling tour that costs $150 (USD), the individual will only be allowed to pay $100 in USD—the remaining $50 must be paid with credit card, Mexican pesos, or wire transfer.

● Certain businesses may not accept U.S. dollars at all, only credit cards and/or Mexican pesos.

to your stateroom. They may be used to present extra gratuities and/or receipts for prepaid tips.

Automated Teller Machines may be available in ports of call, but there are none on the ship. Be sure the machine dispenses U.S. currency before you use it.

Smoking

All Disney ships are, for the most part, smoke-free zones. Smoking is allowed on stateroom verandahs (so you may get a whiff of your neighbors' smoke if your door is open).

On the *Magic* and *Wonder*, smoking is also permitted on the starboard side of open-air Decks 9 and 10 (excluding the Mickey Pool area) and outdoors on Deck 4, starboard side from 6 P.M. to 6 A.M. On *Dream* and the *Fantasy*, smoking is permitted on the port side of the deck area outside of Meridian lounge (located on Deck 12, aft), the port side of Currents lounge (Deck 13, forward), and on the port side of Deck 4, aft, between 6 P.M. and 6 A.M.

Telephone Calls

All staterooms have phones with ship-to-shore capability. Rates range from about $7–$9.50 per minute (subject to change). Toll-free and collect calls can't be placed from ship phones. Wireless service is available in staterooms (fees apply). Be sure to check with your carrier for rates (see How to Call the Ship on page 50). Some ports have pay phones (you will need an international calling card).

Tipping

Some servers, such as bartenders, get an automatic 15 percent gratuity each time you call upon their services. Leave more if you deem the service to be outstanding. That said, folks such as your dining room servers and stateroom host or hostess rely on guests to tip them appropriately. Gratuities are prepaid at the time the cruise reservation is made. Extra gratuities may be charged to your guest folio during the cruise. If you prefer to pay in cash, inform Guest Services at the beginning of the cruise. If a server goes above and beyond, you may add more than the standard 15 percent. Conversely, if he or she doesn't live up to expectations, you may reduce the amount (this situation has never happened to us). Go to the Guest Services desk to make any necessary modifications. Below is a guide to how much gratuity is given to whom. (Guests in Concierge Suites should use their discretion when presenting a gratuity to the concierge.)

PER GUEST/ PER CRUISE	Dining Room Server	Dining Room Assistant Server	Dining Room Head Server	Stateroom Host/Hostess
3-NIGHT	$12	$9	$3	$12
4-NIGHT	$16	$12	$4	$16
5-NIGHT	$20	$15	$5	$20
6-NIGHT	$24	$18	$6	$24
7-NIGHT	$28	$21	$7	$28
8-NIGHT	$32	$24	$8	$32
10-NIGHT	$40	$30	$10	$40
11-NIGHT	$44	$33	$11	$44
14-NIGHT	$56	$42	$14	$56
15-NIGHT	$60	$45	$15	$60

ALL ABOARD

The moment you cross the gangway, you'll realize this vessel is no ordinary home away from home. Step into the grand, multi-story atrium, and, amidst the happy hubbub, your presence is made known in dramatic fashion—with a heartfelt announcement for all to hear. And so begins your high-seas adventure.

The *Disney Magic*, *Wonder*, *Dream*, and *Fantasy* rank among the world's finest ocean-going vessels. The ships are casually elegant and designed to capture the majesty of early ocean liners. They're equipped to satisfy most cruisers, with a mix of traditional seafaring diversions and classic Disney touches. Though some theming and entertainment vary from ship to ship, the accommodations and amenities are similar. As is the service, which is expertly provided by a cast of thousands (representing dozens of countries). All staterooms aboard the quartet of ships are a cut above normal cruising quarters—with an average of 25 percent more space than industry standard. The ships were designed to lure families and grown-ups without offspring to entirely different recreational areas. So, cast aside any preconceived notions you may have about cruising, and expect the unexpected. And don't forget to bring a camera!

Checking In

No matter where it is they call home—be it Bangkok or Boca—all Disney Cruise Line guests begin their respective journeys by checking in at a port terminal. Most Bahamas- and Caribbean-bound guests leaving from Port Canaveral check in at the "A" Terminal. Guests may choose from several different queues at check-in: concierge, Castaway Club (for repeat guests), and general check-in. Guests leaving from Miami check in at Port of Miami Cruise Terminal. For information on other ports the ships may visit throughout 2014, go to *www.disneycruise.com* or call 800-910-3659.

Though no one may board the ship until 1 P.M., guests are welcome to arrive earlier—and guests who check in online get assigned times in advance. (All guests must board by 4 P.M.) The terminal has restrooms and ample seating to relax in while waiting to board.

(At Port Canaveral, Florida, there's also a nifty model of the ship to give you a preview of the real thing.) And, if little ones get antsy, there's lots of room for them to roam around, plus a TV that runs a loop of Disney cartoons. Mickey Mouse and his friends occasionally greet guests in the terminal, too.

Okay, we may have gotten ahead of ourselves. Before you can enter the main part of the terminal, all members of your party must go through a security checkpoint. It's a lot like airport security, so save the holey socks for the second day of your trip (you may be asked to remove your shoes, along with jackets, glasses, belts, etc.). Since kids must go through the security check, too, we recommend having snacks and games to entertain them while you wait (in case the line is more than a few minutes

long). Once you've cleared security, your whole party needs to go to the check-in counter so security photos may be taken.

At the counter, you will be asked to present a valid passport for yourself and each member of your party (see page 33). This is also where you'll be asked for all of your completed cruise paperwork (which can also be completed via the Internet at *www.disneycruise.com* under the "My Online Check-in" section; be sure to select your port arrival time, print and sign the forms, and remember to bring them

with you) and a major credit card. This card will be the one to which all of your extra cruise expenses are charged. If you'd like to split expenses with another guest staying in your room, it is possible to register two credit cards. Once the cruise begins, you'll use your stateroom key—aka Key to the World—card to make purchases and to open your stateroom door. The card also serves as ID for debarking and reboarding purposes (though all ports of call also require a photo ID such as a driver's license for guests over age 18). If you'd prefer that any member of your party not have charging privileges, advise a representative at check-in (or indicate your preference when you check in online).

Once the check-in process is complete, take a peek at your watch. Is it before 1 P.M.? If so, sit back, relax, and wait for the boarding process to begin. You could

AHOY, MATEY!

Throughout the cruise, you may hear a few terms with which you're unfamiliar. To avoid confusion, here's a little nautical talk 101:

AFT—directional term meaning toward the back (stern) of a ship

BOW—the front of a ship

BRIDGE—the place from which the captain and helmsman navigate a ship and give orders

BUOY—a floating object used to mark a channel or something lying under the water

DECK—a platform stretching along a ship

FORWARD—a directional term meaning toward the front of a ship

FUNNEL—a large, hollow tube or pipe through which exhaust from a ship's engine can escape

GALLEY—the kitchen on a ship

HULL—the outer frame or body of a ship

KNOT—the measure of a ship's speed. One knot is one nautical mile per hour.

MIDSHIP—referring to the area in the middle of a ship

PORT—the left-hand side of a ship (facing forward)

PORTHOLE—a window in the side of a ship

STARBOARD—the right-hand side of a ship (facing forward)

STATEROOM—living quarters for passengers and crew on board a ship (aka cabin)

STERN—the rear end of a ship

HOT TIP

The *Disney Magic* recently got a magical makeover. Disney Cruise Line's original ship, relaunched in late 2013, boasts a bevy of new dining, entertainment, and recreational opportunities. Tops on the "must-do" list? The 3-story AquaDunk waterslide! There are plenty of other ways to make a splash on board, too. Look for new kids' activities, a re-imagined adult fun zone, a grander grand lobby, roomier staterooms, and lots of other pixie-dusted programs. For details, keep reading and visit *www.disneycruise.com*.

also use the extra time to register kids for shipboard youth activities. If it's after 1 P.M., wait for your boarding number to be called (every party receives one when they check in). When your number's called, grab the kids and your day bags and head for the gangway. All aboard!

The Boarding Experience

After you slip through the entry portal, you'll enter a subdued hallway. This is where you may have your "pre-cruise" photo taken by a Cruise Line photographer. Try to look as stressed out as possible. That'll make the "post-cruise" shots that much more enjoyable. (You can buy copies of this photo on the ship later that day or soon after.)

On the far side of the photo-op area, there's a door leading to a covered, air-conditioned gangway. Cross that and you'll find yourself deposited smack-dab in the middle of the ship's grand lobby. A dramatic backdrop for a dramatic entrance.

Depending on the time (staterooms are usually ready by 1:30 P.M.) and your level of starvation, you may want to make a quick stop, change, and head to Parrot Cay or Beach Blanket Buffet (on the *Wonder*), Carioca's or Cabanas (on the *Magic*), or Enchanted Garden or Cabanas (*Dream* and *Fantasy*) for lunch. The pools are usually open throughout the afternoon. If you arrive as the time nears 2:30 P.M., skip the stateroom stop and make a beeline for the nearest eatery serving lunch—it's usually served until 3:30 P.M. After that, a visit to the stateroom is imperative, as the mandatory safety drill

takes place at 3:45 P.M. on the *Dream* and *Fantasy* and at 4 P.M. on the *Magic* and *Wonder*. (For the drill on the safety drill, see page 83.)

Once the safety drill is complete, you may head back to your room to prepare for the sailaway deck celebration known as Adventures Away (*Magic* and *Wonder*) and Sailing Away (*Dream* and

HOT TIP

If you or a member of your party misplaces a Key to the World card while on board, head to the Guest Services desk on Deck 3. They can issue a new one (free of charge).

Fantasy). If you've got an early dinner seating, this is the ideal time to change into your evening attire.

Finally, we simply cannot overemphasize the importance of making reservations for spa treatments and for Palo and Remy (adults-only eateries) as early as possible. (It's best to book before the trip begins, via *www. disneycruise.com*.) Make last-minute spa appointments at the spa itself. For Palo, which begins accepting reservations at about 1 P.M.

on day one of the cruise, head for Fathoms (*Magic*), WaveBands (*Wonder*), or D Lounge (*Dream* and *Fantasy*). Reservations for Remy (upscale dining for grown-ups on the *Dream* and *Fantasy*) may be made here, too. Plan to register children for youth activities in the terminal or soon after boarding (see pages 111–116 for details).

Ship Shape

The *Disney Magic*, *Wonder*, *Dream*, and *Fantasy* are

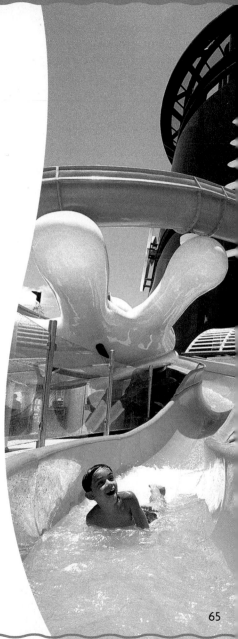

equipped to satisfy even the most savvy of cruisers, with a mix of traditional seafaring diversions and unmistakable Disney touches. The ships' classic exteriors recall the majesty of early ocean liners. Guests enter a three-story atrium, where traditional definitions of elegance expand to include bronze character statues and subtle cutout character silhouettes along a grand staircase. Recreation areas are designed to draw families and kid-free adults to different parts of the ship. By day, fun in the sun alternates with touring, lunch, indoor distractions, and perhaps even a little bingo action. Evenings give way to sunset sail-away celebrations, themed dining experiences, and theatrical extravaganzas. What follows is a description of the ships' accommodations, shops, restaurants, lounges, pools, entertainment, and a whole lot more.

Decked Out

Here's the deck-by-deck rundown, from top to bottom (the first section of this deck-specific data refers to the *Magic* and *Wonder*; the section that follows covers the *Dream* and *Fantasy*):

MAGIC AND WONDER

Deck 11

On the *Magic* and *Wonder*, you'll find the teen club Vibe. This venue is exclusively available to teenage guests (see page 95).

Deck 10

Known as the Wide World of Sports Deck (*Magic* and *Wonder*), we find it a perfect late-night place to watch the moon and stars. There's also a basketball court. And this is one of the best places to be during the sail-away party. (For more on the sports deck, see page 121.) Palo is here, too (see page 90). For adults only, this dining spot offers fine cuisine and panoramic views. The *Disney Wonder* has the Outlook Café, too.

Deck 9

Pampering, Disney style, can be enjoyed in the soothing Spa & Salon (Vista on the *Wonder*, Senses on the *Magic*). At the spa, guests may experience treatments in the spa villas, as well as a little Rest & Relaxation on the outdoor verandah. Fitness-minded folk can get a one-on-one fitness consultation. There's lots of exercise equipment, saunas, a steam room, and spa treatments. Personal training is offered too. (For details, see page 125.)

Deck 9 is also where you'll find the ships' pools: Quiet Cove (for adults); Mickey's Pool (*Wonder* kids' pool), and AquaDunk and AquaLab (waterslide and kids' water zone on the *Magic*), plus a kids' slide and a splash zone for little ones; and Goofy's Pool (for families). This deck is also home to Cove Cafe (coffee bar for adults), Quarter Masters (arcade), Goofy's Galley, Pinocchio's Pizzeria, Pluto's Dog House, and Topsider (*Wonder*) or Cabanas (*Magic*).

PRINCESS AUTOGRAPH SESSION

The excitement builds as kids and their parents gather in line for the chance to add treasured signatures to their autograph books. Offered at least once per cruise, this event features regals such as Cinderella, Snow White, Tiana, and Aurora, who make their entrance and begin a parade. Young admirers file past—many dressed in princess outfits of their own—stopping to ask each Disney Princess for an autograph. Don't forget the camera. Note that cruise staff members are on hand to make sure the line keeps moving. Check the *Personal Navigator* to see which princesses are scheduled to appear, as well as for dates and times.

Deck 5

Kids have the run of more than half of this deck. It's one of the largest dedicated areas of children's space afloat, with comprehensive, interest-specific activities. (For details, turn to page 111.)

The Buena Vista Theatre is also located here on all ships. A full-screen cinema with Dolby Sound and 3-D technology, it offers films every day, featuring Disney's animated classics and first-run releases. It hosts guest speakers on occasion, too.

Deck 4

Here you'll find the Walt Disney Theatre, Shutters (photo shop), and Animator's Palate (restaurant). The *Magic* has D Lounge, and the *Wonder* offers Studio Sea. This is also a lovely deck on which to enjoy a leisurely stroll, a jog, or a nice nap.

The Walt Disney Theatre is a grand venue that features

one of the most sophisticated show settings at sea or on land. The formal theater boasts extraordinary lighting and technical facilities, and showcases up to three distinct Broadway-style musical productions (each with a decidedly Disney touch) during each cruise.

Animator's Palate is a cheerful restaurant that offers creatively prepared cuisine in a room that features a colorful masterpiece of synchronized light and sound. Deck 4 on the *Magic* and *Wonder* is also the place where you can find a duo of shops selling Disney Cruise Line-themed clothing for the family, character merchandise, collectibles, specialty items, jewelry, and sundries (see pages 117–119 for more details).

Deck 3

This is the place for dining and dancing on the *Magic* and *Wonder*; After Hours

(*Magic*) and Route 66 (*Wonder*) are adult-oriented evening entertainment districts that offer themed clubs (see page 101 for details). Fathoms (*Magic*) and WaveBands (*Wonder*) often have themed parties—

GUEST SERVICES DESK

As much as we like to think this book has all the answers, questions will likely arise on board. If so, head to the Guest Services Desk (Deck 3, midship). This is also the spot to go to secure extra copies of the *Personal Navigator*, color-coded luggage tags (for use on the last day of the cruise), and postage stamps. Should you have any type of problem while on board, bring it to their attention. More often than not, they will resolve the issue in a matter of minutes.

and don't forget the room's biggest attraction . . . bingo! There is a sports bar (Diversions on the *Wonder*, O'Gill's on the *Magic*); Radar Trap (*Wonder*) and Up Beat (*Magic*) are duty-free shops; Keys (on the *Magic*) and Cadillac Lounge (on the *Wonder*) are casual yet sophisticated places to relax and listen to live piano music; and Promenade Lounge is a place to enjoy

a drink and hear music (on the *Magic* and *Wonder*). Adjacent to the Promenade Lounge is the Internet Cafe. Also here are Parrot Cay (*Wonder*), an island-inspired restaurant; Carioca's (*Magic*), an eatery inspired by Rio de Janeiro; and Lumière's, serving continental cuisine (on the *Magic*). Lumière's has a French flair and a beautiful

DISNEY CRUISE LINE GIFTS

Whether you'll be celebrating a special occasion or simply consider the cruise a special occasion unto itself, you may want to have a gift item delivered to your stateroom as an added surprise. Among the items that can be pre-ordered by calling 800-601-8455, or visiting *disneycruise. com* are flower arrangements, food and beverage packages, wine selections, cakes, and Disney Cruise Line merchandise. Orders must be placed at least 48 business hours before sail date.

HOT TIP

All rooms have small safes. There is no charge. (Lock it with a number code you select, and unlock it using the same code.) Note that the safe isn't big enough for iPads or laptops.

mural of Disney's *Beauty and the Beast*. Its counterpart on the *Wonder*, Triton's, has an underwater-like setting of blues, greens, and purples. Guest Services is also on this deck and is open 24 hours a day. The Port Adventures (aka shore excursions) desk is nearby.

Deck 2
All Disney ships have staterooms on this deck. Mid-ship is where you'll find Edge, the tween-only hangout for 11- to 14-year-olds. The interactive play area has a lab with child-friendly computers, video game consoles, arts and crafts tables, flat-panel TVs, and comfy couches. Kids can also sing karaoke, go on scavanger hunts, and more.

Deck 1
This is where you will find the ship's Medical Center. There are some staterooms here, too.

CHANNEL SURFING

Each Disney ship carries up to 21 different television stations. Rather than chastise you for watching TV when there's about a million better things to do on board, here's a listing of some of the channels you may find (some are commercial, some strictly in-house). Note that all channels are subject to blackouts:

Entertainment Guide
View from the Bridge
Safety/Environmental Video
Shopping Channel
Good Morning America at Sea
What's Afloat
Port Adventures/Debark Info
ABC
Disney Channel
ESPN International
ESPN
ESPN 2
Have a Laugh Cartoons
Toon Disney
Music Video Channel
Shows from the Walt Disney Theatre
Company Clips
Disney Vacation Club
ABC Sitcoms
ABC Movies
Disney Animated Features
Disney/Pixar Animated Features

Decks 1, 2, 5, 6, 7, and 8
Shipboard accommodations are spread over these decks.

DREAM AND FANTASY

Deck 14
The pinnacle of these sister ships, Deck 14 is the site of Outlook, a lounge that offers sweeping ocean vistas in addition to cocktails.

Deck 13
Here you'll find Edge (tweens hangout), Currents (open-air bar), and Goofy's Sports Deck. This is also where concierge guests may enjoy a private sundeck. On the *Fantasy*, there's Satellite Falls—a waterfall-endowed wading pool for guests ages 18 and older.

Deck 12
This is the home of the luxurious Senses Spa & Salon (which extends to Deck 11), Meridian (lounge), Palo, and Remy (both are upscale eateries for grown-ups; Remy is *trés* indulgent). Grown-up guests may sip spirits and soft drinks at Waves bar. Deck 12 is also the site of AquaLab (*Fantasy*) and mini-golf and the AquaDuck water coaster (*Dream* and *Fantasy*).

Deck 11
On the *Dream* and *Fantasy*, this a destination deck for hungry guests: Cove Cafe (coffee bar for adults); Cabanas (buffet); and Flo's Cafe, a quick-service eatery comprised of three stations (Luigi's Pizza, Tow Mater's Grill, and Fillmore's Favorites). Also on this deck are Eye Scream and Frozone Treats. Deck 11 is home to Mickey's Pool, Quiet Cove Pool, Donald's Pool, Nemo's Reef (splash zone), and Arr-cade.

Deck 10, 9, 8, 7, 6, and 2
On the *Dream* and *Fantasy*, these decks are devoted primarily to staterooms.

Deck 5

Deck 5 is kid-central—and they wouldn't want it any other way! In addition to the It's a Small World Nursery (see page 115), this is the site of the kids' programming areas known as Disney's Oceaneer Club and Lab (page 113), as well as Vibe (teen club). It's also the site of the Buena Vista (movie) Theatre's balcony. Bibbidi Bobbidi Boutique and Pirate's League (princess and pirate makeovers) are here, too (*Dream* and *Fantasy*).

Deck 4

Here you'll find the Buena Vista Theatre (movies), Vista Gallery (art), and Shutters (photo shop). The Walt Disney Theatre is a grand venue that showcases Broadway-style productions (with a distinct Disney flair) during each cruise. This venue extends to Deck 5.

Also found on Deck 4 of the *Dream* and *Fantasy*:

D Lounge (family lounge and nightclub) and the ships' respective adults-only entertainment zones. Among the offerings in The District on the *Dream*: Skyline (lounge with panoramic views of various city skylines), District Lounge, Evolution (dance club), a sports bar called 687, and Pink (a champagne lounge). On the *Fantasy*, expect to find these spots in the Europa entertainment district: La Piazza (a lounge that celebrates Italian plazas), Skyline (bar with panoramic views of famous cities), O'Gill's (sports pub), Ooh La La (an elegant champagne bar inspired by a French boudoir), and The Tube (a dance club with a London Underground motif).

Deck 3

This deck is home to the Art Deco–inspired lobby, the Walt Disney Theatre (stage shows), a bar, shops, and restaurants. The Bon

HOT TIP

The midship elevators are the most crowded throughout the day—especially at mealtimes. Try to use the forward and aft elevators whenever possible.

Deck 2
This is the site of the Enchanted Garden eatery.

Decks 2, and 5–12
Shipboard accommodations are spread over these decks.

Deck 1
The ship's Medical Center is on Deck 1.

Staterooms

Voyage lounge is on the port side of the grand lobby. Beyond this imbibing zone are the ship's shops: Mickey's Mainsail, Whitecaps, and Sea Treasures.

Animator's Palate is a cheerful restaurant that offers creatively prepared cuisine in an impeccably designed dining room (for additional information on the restaurant, see page 84).

Other Deck 3 dining options include Royal Palace (*Dream*) and Royal Court (*Fantasy*).

Guest Services, which is open around the clock, is also located on Deck 3.

The accommodations on Disney's ships range from standard inside rooms to suites with verandahs. All staterooms aboard each ship are a cut above the standard cruising cabin. On average, these staterooms offer substantially more space, most have a split bath (see the sidebar on the facing page), and most of them are outside rooms with ocean vistas—many with verandahs.

Staterooms are decorated in a nautical theme with

natural woods and imported tiles. Universal amenities include a TV, Wave phones that allow you to call or text another member of your party while on board (two phones are included per stateroom—extras may be rented), telephone with voice mail (and ship-to-shore capability), an in-room safe, a room service menu (in the Directory of Services book), and lots of drawer space. The *Dream* and *Fantasy* also come equipped with small refrigerators. (On the *Magic* and *Wonder*, there's a "cooling box" instead of a fridge. It's chilly enough to store most perishables, but not medication.) After that, different types of accommodations— which are labeled by category—offer different amenities (verandahs are included in the square footage):

MAGIC AND WONDER

CATEGORIES 11A–11C
Standard inside staterooms. They have a queen bed or two twin beds, a single convertible sofa, a privacy divider, and a bath. Each room measures 184 square feet and sleeps up to 3 or 4.

CATEGORY 10A–10C
Deluxe inside staterooms. These accommodations are similar to those found in categories 11A–11C but have 214 square feet of space and a split bath.

WHAT'S A SPLIT BATH?

In most staterooms ranging from category 4 through 10, accommodations come with a "split" bathroom. It's really like having two small bathrooms, side by side. One has a sink and a toilet. The other has a sink and a tub/shower.

LAUNDRY FACILITIES

Laundry and dry cleaning services are available for a fee. Items will be picked up and delivered to your stateroom. If you'd rather go the self-service laundry route, you can do so in one of several Guest Laundry Rooms. Here you'll find washers, dryers, and ironing equipment. (Due to safety concerns, the laundry room is the only place in which iron use is permitted.) There is no fee to use an iron. Machines run about two bucks a load. Laundry detergent may be purchased here, too. At press time, a small box cost about $1. Simply wave your Key to the World card and charge it to your stateroom account.

HOT TIP

Every day brings with it a new "drink of the day." It's a specialty cocktail served at the bars and lounges on board. The beverage will be noted in the *Personal Navigator*. It is often available at a special price.

CATEGORIES 9A–9D

Deluxe ocean-view staterooms. These come with a queen or two twin beds, a single convertible sofa, a privacy divider, and split bath. Rooms on Deck 1 have two small windows, while those on Deck 2 and above feature one large window. Each room is 214 square feet. It sleeps up to 3 or 4 guests.

CATEGORIES 5A–5C, 6A, AND 7A

Deluxe ocean-view staterooms with verandahs. Each has one queen or two twin-size beds, a single convertible sofa, a privacy divider, split bath, and a verandah. These rooms are 268 square feet (including the verandah) and sleep up to 4. Category 7A has an enclosed "Navigator's Verandah," a private balcony with nautical touches. The verandahs in 5A–5C are open, while those in 6A feature a solid whitewall verandah. Accommodations are otherwise the same.

CATEGORY 4A, 4B, and 4E
Deluxe ocean-view family staterooms with verandah. This room type has a queen or two twin beds, a single convertible sofa, and a bed that pulls down from the wall. There is a privacy divider, split bath, and open verandah (verandahs in the aft area are not open). It covers 304 square feet (including verandah) and sleeps up to 5.

CATEGORY 00T
Concierge one-bedroom suites with verandah. These have a queen bed, an area with a double convertible sofa, and a pull-down bed, two full baths, walk-in closet, wet bar, DVD player, open verandah (except for the aft-area staterooms), and concierge service. The suite is 614

square feet (including the verandah) and sleeps up to 4 or 5 guests.

CATEGORY 00S
Concierge two-bedroom suites with verandahs. These suites come with a queen bed, a sleeper-sofa, and a pull-down bed. There are 2.5 baths, a whirlpool tub, walk-in closets, a DVD player, unstocked wet bar, verandah, and concierge service. The suite measures 945 square feet and sleeps up to 7.

CATEGORY 00R
Concierge royal suite with verandah. Comes with a queen bed in one bedroom, two twin beds in a second bedroom, and two ceiling pull-down upper berths. There are 2.5 baths, a whirlpool tub in the master bedroom, a living room, media library (with a pull-down bed), dining salon, pantry, unstocked wet bar, walk-in closets, DVD

player, private verandah, and concierge service. The suite measures 1,029 square feet and sleeps up to 7.

DREAM AND FANTASY

CATEGORIES 11A–11C

Standard inside staterooms. They have a queen, a single convertible sofa, upper berth pull-down bed (in some), and a bath with a tub and shower. Each room measures 169 square feet and sleeps up to 3 (category 11C) or 4 (categories 11A and 11B). They also have "magical portholes" (see Category 10A).

CATEGORY 10A

Deluxe inside staterooms. These accommodations are similar to those found in categories 11A–11C, but have 204 square feet and sleep up to 3 to 4 guests. They also have split baths, plus a bit of technological and artistic wizardry known as "magical portholes." These

beauties have a real-time digital view that could be seen from a real porthole at any given time of day or night, and they feature visits from animated Disney characters. Most folks say they forget they are in an inside stateroom—the effect is that convincing.

CATEGORIES 9A–9D

Deluxe ocean-view staterooms. These come with a queen bed, a single convertible sofa, upper berth pull-down bed (in some), split bath, and porthole. Each room is 204 square feet and sleeps up to 3 or 4 guests.

CATEGORIES 8A–8D

Deluxe family ocean-view staterooms. These come with a queen bed, a single convertible sofa, wall pull-down bed (in most) or upper berth pull-down bed, and a split bath with a round tub (in most). Each stateroom features a large porthole window with built-in seating, measures 241 square feet, and sleeps up to 3 or 5. The 8A stateroom has two large porthole windows but does not have a split bath.

CATEGORIES 5A–5E, 6A–6B, 7A

Deluxe ocean-view staterooms with verandahs. Each has one queen bed, a single convertible sofa, pull-down bed if sleeping 4, a split bath, and a verandah. These rooms are 246 square feet (including the verandah) and sleep up to 3 or 4. The verandahs in 5A and the aft rooms of 6A and 6B feature whitewall verandahs. 7A rooms either have a smaller verandah or an obstructed view. 5E staterooms have larger verandahs and are all aft. Accommodations are otherwise the same.

CATEGORY 4A–4E

Deluxe ocean-view family staterooms with verandah. This room type has a queen bed, a single convertible sofa, upper berth pull-down bed (in most), a split bath with a round tub (in most) and a shower, and a verandah. Each stateroom is 299 square feet (including verandah) and sleeps up to 5. The verandahs in 4E rooms are twice the size of the verandahs in other Category 4 staterooms.

CATEGORY 00V

Concierge Deluxe family ocean-view staterooms with verandah. This room type has a queen bed, a double convertible sofa, upper berth pull-down bed, full bath (with vanity, sink, round tub, and shower), half bath (vanity, sink, and toilet), a verandah, and concierge service. Each stateroom covers 306 square feet (including verandah) and sleeps up to 5 guests.

CATEGORY 00T

Concierge one-bedroom suites with verandah. These posh suites have a bedroom with a queen bed, a living area with a double convertible sofa, and a single pull-down bed in the living room, walk-in closet, two full bathrooms (with a whirlpool in the master bath), verandah, and concierge service. The suite is 622 square feet (including the verandah) and sleeps up to 5 guests.

CATEGORY 00R

Concierge royal suite with verandah. Comes with a queen bed in the master bedroom, 1 wall pull-down double bed and 1 wall pull-down single bed in the living room. There are 2 full bathrooms, including a master bath with double sinks, rain shower, and whirlpool tub (there is also a whirlpool tub on the verandah), plus living room, media library, open dining

A TENDER SUBJECT

Some ports require a process called "tendering." This means, rather than pulling right up to a dock, the ship will pull close to port and drop anchor. Ferries take guests back and forth to shore. It's an efficient system, but it could knock you for a loop if you're not expecting it—especially if you've got an early excursion booked. In this case, you may have to leave a bit earlier than you originally anticipated. That is accounted for in the "meet time" for all excursions.

salon, pantry, wet bar, walk-in closet, verandah, and concierge service. The suite measures 1,781 square feet and sleeps up to 5.

The Personal Navigator

There's just so much to see and do on a daily basis, a passenger could easily become overwhelmed, if not downright discombobulated. Not to worry. An in-house publication called the *Personal Navigator* will help you make the most of every day. Updated daily and delivered to all staterooms, the publication is a comprehensive listing of a day's onboard activities, events, and entertainment.

We simply cannot overemphasize the importance of the daily *Personal Navigator*. It is a truly indispensable tool. When you get your hands on it (the first one should be waiting for you in your stateroom), drop everything and read it cover to cover. In addition to listing the lineup of activities scheduled for the rest of the day (which on day one may include the Adventures Away sail-away party), it'll provide many other handy bits of information. For instance, in the upper-right corner of the front page, you'll find the suggested evening attire for that day. It changes from day to day, so be sure to note it. It also gives the time and location of Disney character appearances, any points of interest the ship may have scheduled, a notification of any time zone changes, as well as any special offers at

shops or lounges. Keep an eye out for discounts on Internet use, too. From this pamphlet, you'll also glean the times of sunrise and sunset, should you aspire to be on an observation deck for Mother Nature's daily presentations.

Dining

A Disney cruise is not the place to count calories—although most special dietary needs can be accommodated upon request. There's no shortage of rations on these ships. If your tastes are simple (say, a hot dog poolside) or sublime (how does a juicy filet mignon, courtesy of Palo, sound?), rest assured you'll never be hungry. Or understimulated, for that matter, as many of the restaurants are downright entertaining. And, thanks to a system called "rotational dining," you will get to experience three restaurants, all the while being made to feel like a VIP by your serving staff. That means you'll eat at a different one of the three main restaurants each evening, often with the same table guests, and enjoy the services of the same

DAY ONE SAFETY DRILL

It's nearly 4 P.M. You've just started to unpack. You're weary from your journey. And all you want to do is plop down on a poolside lounge chair. Hold that thought. Before you get started on that much needed R&R, you've got a job to do. A very important, attendance-mandatory, skip-it-and-you've-broken-the-law job. It's called an Assembly Drill, and maritime law requires that all passengers participate prior to leaving your home port.

The drill is meant to prepare you for the unlikely event that you'd have to board a lifeboat. It sounds simple enough: Once you've found the life jackets (they're on the top shelf of the stateroom closet), try them on to make sure you know how to get the perfect fit. After that, place the jackets back where you found them, as they are not needed during the safety drill. Then, listen for the ship's general alarm (7 short blasts followed by one long one). As soon as you hear the alarm, make your way to your assigned assembly station (you'll find information on your assembly station on the back of your stateroom door and also on your Key to the World card). Make sure to bring your Key to the World cards with you, as these will be used to check your party in for the mandatory roll call.

Once the drill is completed (figure about 20 minutes), you've done your job and now can start to relax (finally) and join the fun on board.

FYI: The Disney Cruise Line safety drill has been rated number one by the United States Power Squadrons, a nonprofit organization that is dedicated to making boating as safe as possible. Good to know!

waitstaff. Your serving team gets to know you, as well as your likes and dislikes, very well. The system, which is unique to Disney Cruise Line, tends to get the thumbs-up from cruise veterans and newcomers alike. The only exceptions to the rule are Palo and Remy, the adults-only, reservations-necessary restaurants. (For details on Palo, see page 90; for Remy, refer to page 92.)

How do you know where to go on which night? Easy. A ticket with details will be placed in your stateroom. Don't forget to check the day's *Personal Navigator* to note the style of attire for the evening.

TABLE SERVICE

The *Magic* and *Wonder* each have four table-service restaurants, while the *Dream* and *Fantasy* have five apiece. Three restaurants on each ship are included in Disney's unique "rotational dining"

system. They all serve dinner, but check the *Personal Navigator* for hours and meals served at each spot for the rest of the day.

Animator's Palate

The *pièce de résistance*—as far as Disney creativity goes—is without a doubt Animator's Palate, a place where diners not only have to decide what to eat, but also what to watch! Simple surprises abound at each stage of the evening meal. There is an Animator's Palate eatery on each of the four ships, but the dining experience varies depending on which ship you are sailing on. The Animator's Palate experience on the *Wonder* is a culinary journey—from black and white to full color: Upon entering the monochromatic room, you will be led to your table and asked for your order. Note the soft background music and the black-and-white sketches along the wall. While you're doing so, drinks and appetizers will be served. If you ignore this distraction and keep your gaze fixed on the walls, you may notice a bit of color creeping into that sketch of Cinderella. By the time the entrées make their entrance, the room is ablaze in living color. The music tends to get a bit livelier by this point, too. You may even notice that your waitstaff becomes more colorful toward meal's end.

The menu on *Wonder* has featured items such as salmon wrapped in phyllo dough, beef tenderloin, and other tempting choices. If they're available, we recommend starting with the butternut squash soup and capping it off with a slice of double-fudge chocolate cake. The ice cream is tempting, too.

If you are sailing on the *Magic*, *Dream*, or the *Fantasy*, your Animator's Palate meal will be a somewhat

HOT TIP

At table-service restaurants, a gratuity of 15 percent is automatically added to the bill for alcoholic beverages. At bars and lounges, a gratuity is added for all drinks (including soft drinks).

different experience. Like its namesake on the *Wonder*, this restaurant's decor was inspired by the magic of Disney and Pixar animation. It's teeming with everything you'd expect to find inside an actual animator's studio: character sketches, paintbrushes, colored pencils, computer workstations, and other tools of the animation trade. Scenes and characters from Disney films adorn the walls, and that totally awesome, animated turtle called Crush actually *interacts* with diners on the *Dream*.

The *Fantasy* and *Magic* one-up their sister ships

85

with a dinner show called Animation Magic. Hosted by Sorcerer Mickey, the interactive experience encourages guests to express themselves with a drawing—and over the course of dinner, they'll witness as their drawings are brought to life through the magic of Disney animation. Every show is a smash hit with artists of all ages. Crush the turtle may appear here on some nights, too.

Menu items here have included the Animator's trio of veal, including a pulled shank and tortellacci pasta with a sun-dried tomato and sage reduction, garnished with a potato crisp. The featured dessert is a decadent chocolate brownie cheesecake with whipped cream and raspberry coulis.

Enchanted Garden

This picturesque spot, which is located on the *Dream* and *Fantasy*, seems to be truly enchanted, as the immersive, outdoorsy environment transforms from day to night over the course of your dinner.

Breakfast, served buffet style, is offered on select days of each cruise. Ditto for lunch. The daily dinner is a four-course affair of seasonal selections. For an extra charge (plus gratuity), guests may enjoy bar drinks, bottled water, and specialty coffee. Soft drinks (coffee, soda, fruit juice, milk, and tea) carry no charge. This eatery is on Deck 2, midship.

Lumière's

Located on the *Magic* only, this elegant spot provides fine dining in a setting inspired by Disney's *Beauty and the Beast*. The sprawling dining room is elegant and softly lit, though a bit more raucous than its cosmopolitan contemporaries. Note that the later seating is usually a bit more sedate (fewer small kids).

Menu selections at dinner have included crispy roasted

duck breast with braised napa cabbage, and aged Angus beef tenderloin. Vegetarians can opt for the porcini-mushroom-stuffed pasta in a vegetable broth. And waist-watchers won't feel cheated by the grilled marinated tofu. For dessert, consider the crème brûlée or soufflé. No-sugar-added selections are available, as well: chocolate cheesecake and an apple-cinnamon fruit dish served with a fresh-baked brownie.

Triton's

Passengers aboard the *Wonder* may dine in the elegant Triton's, where the specialty of the house is seafood. The ocean theme is enhanced by subtly changing lighting with every course, the room getting more under-the-sea-like as the meal progresses. Menu items have included French onion soup, three-cheese lobster macaroni, seared sea bass, and braised lamb shank. For dessert, there's chocolate mousse, Grand Marnier soufflé, sundaes, and more.

Parrot Cay

This tropical spot, which is located on the *Wonder* and is pronounced Parrot *KEY*, is certainly one of the most colorful spaces you'll ever dine in. Done up in vibrant shades of orange, green, blue, and yellow, it boasts a rainbow of cleverly formed napkin displays at each table. The island-like feel has been complemented by such dinner dishes as pan-seared grouper, poached halibut

with clams and mussels, Caribbean roasted chicken, and mixed grill. Kids tend to appreciate the macaroni and cheese, a Disney specialty. Dessert-wise, expect the likes of lemon meringue pie with kumquat sauce, chocolate s'more vanilla cake, and French toast banana bread. This is exclusive to *Wonder*.

Carioca's

This vibrant restaurant (on the *Magic*) is a tribute to the city of Rio de Janeiro (the second-largest city in Brazil). The name of the eatery, however, honors José Carioca—one of the stars of *The Three Caballeros*. The menu has featured items with Latin-infused flavors such as adobo-rubbed rack of lamb; lobster *croquetas* with banana and lentil salad; and lobster, shrimp, and mahi mahi kebabs with black bean rice and *pico de gallo*. Cap off the meal with cream cheese flan with caramel bananas.

Royal Palace/Royal Court

This regal restaurant (Royal Palace on the *Dream* and Royal Court on the *Fantasy*) got its inspiration from classic Disney animated features such as *Sleeping Beauty*, *Beauty and the Beast*, and *Cinderella*. You will find the eatery on Deck 3, midship.

French-inspired, continental cuisine is offered for breakfast, lunch, and dinner. Breakfast is offered on select mornings of each cruise, as is a full-service lunch. A four-course dinner takes place nightly. One of the favorite appetizers at dinner is the escargots gratinés (herb-marinated snails). Grilled beef tenderloin and shrimp is a featured entrée. Vegetarian selections such as mushroom-filled pasta are served, too. And do save room for the "sweet temptations" dessert offering: a trio of peanut butter mousse, mango cheesecake, and vanilla crème brûlée. Yum!

Seating Times and Situations

There are normally two seating sessions for dinner; however, the times vary depending on what itinerary the ship is sailing at the time. The most common times are 5:45 P.M. and 8:15 P.M. If you have a preference, tell your travel agent or reservationist the moment you book your cruise. Requests for any seating cannot be guaranteed. If you get closed out of a preferred seating time, check with Guest Services after boarding. Seating times may open up after boarding. Most seating at table-service restaurants is communal, except at Palo and Remy. If you are traveling as a family with kids, expect to be seated with similar travelers. Adults without kids will be seated together if possible.

Parents of young kids, listen up! There is a dining convenience designed just for you. Dine and Play lets parents with late dinner seatings to

HOT TIP

meals quickly, while serving the grown-ups at a more relaxed pace.

Youth activities counselors arrive in the restaurant 45 minutes after the seating begins, and assign children to groups right there in the dining room. No need for parents to escort junior to Deck 5. (Though they will eventually have to pick the kids up!) Remember, this service is for guests with late dinner seatings only.

Palo

For adults only, Palo is an ideal spot for special celebrations or just a quiet, romantic evening. Offering brunch and dinner, Palo is worth the small surcharge (at press time, prices were $20 for brunch and dinner) to indulge in a five-star dining experience that includes an ocean view.

True to its roots (*palo* means "pole" in Italian), the restaurant has echoes of

check their kids (ages 3–11) into the Youth Activities programs starting about 45 minutes after dinner seating has begun. In other words, after the kids have eaten, they can go play while you finish your meal in a leisurely manner. Neat idea, huh? If you wish to partake of the complimentary Dine and Play service, simply inform your servers upon arrival in the dining room. They will make sure kids get their

Venice, Italy. Masks from that city's *Carnevale* line the walls, and the menu reflects some of the best continental fare you'll find on either side of the Atlantic. For dinner, appetizers include fresh, homemade (and delicious) fritto di calamari and tuna carpaccio—thin slices of tuna brushed with the chef's special lemon olive oil. The entrée menu tempts with selections such as oregano and parmesan-crusted rack of lamb; osso bucco di vitello (slow-roasted center-cut veal shank with gremolata and risotto milanese); and lobster mascarpone ravioli.

A warning: Save room for dessert or you will never forgive yourself. The chocolate soufflé (with hot chocolate and vanilla sauces) is beyond amazing. (The sweet soufflé must be ordered in advance.) The pineapple-and-almond ravioli and Palo's homemade tiramisu yield raves, too.

Brunch at Palo is indeed a special event. (It's offered on cruises of 4 nights or more.) The buffet is so vast that it requires a guided tour (which, happily, you will receive). Expect to sample fruit, salads, seafood, heavenly flatbreads, pastries, made-to-order omelets, fish, and chicken entrées, and more.

HOT TIP

Beer drinkers, take note: If you purchase a refillable mug at the start of the cruise, you will be entitled to discount suds for the duration of your stay on the ship. (You must present the beer card token to net the discount.)

Palo is for diners ages 18 years and older. Reservations can be made at *www.disneycruise.com*; at Fathoms (*Magic*), WaveBands (*Wonder*), or D Lounge (*Dream* and *Fantasy*); or at the restaurant itself starting at approximately 1 P.M. on the first day of a cruise.

NOTE: *Palo offers brunch during some cruises of 4 nights or longer. Shorts, jeans, bathing suits, and tank tops are not acceptable attire for any meal at Palo.*

Remy

For adults (age 18 and older) on the *Dream* and *Fantasy*, Remy is a ritzy, palate-pleasing delight. Considered the most upscale dining experience available on the ship, Remy serves fine French-inspired cuisine for dinner (all cruises) and brunch (on cruises of 4 nights or more). The luxurious dining room has Art Nouveau touches and a rich color scheme. Tables are set with Frette linens, Riedel glassware, Christofle silverware, and custom-created Bernadaud china.

Once the meal is booked and guests are aboard the ship, they can meet with a sommelier in Remy's wine room to pick out wines for their pending feast (for an additional price).

The evening meal begins with a champagne cocktail and continues with 8 to 9 small (delectable) courses. There's nothing more thrilling than a table-side visit from the trolley of international cheeses—except, perhaps, for the wine

HOT TIP

To avoid being charged for canceling a Palo or Remy reservation, you must cancel by 2 P.M. on the day of the reservation.

decanting stations and after-dinner coffee service.

The private Chef's Table experience takes place in a special 8-seat dining room and features *Ratatouille*-inspired decor.

Oenophiles appreciate the lovely Wine Room, which accommodates up to 8 guests. Here, guests dine in a glass-walled room with marble flooring amid 900 bottles of wine.

Reservations are required to dine at Remy, and meals come with a $75-per-person surcharge for dinner and $50 per person for brunch. Reservations may be made online (75 days ahead for first-time cruisers, 90 for Silver Castaway Club members, 105 days ahead for Gold members, and 120 days in advance for concierge guests and Platinum members).

Like its posh neighbor, Palo, Remy also has a dress code. Dinner is a bit more formal here than at Palo:

HOT TIP

Palo and Remy reservations will not appear on your *Personal Navigator*. (It's not *that* personal!) Make sure you don't miss it. There is an extra per-person charge for all meals. Call 800-910-3659 for specifics.

jackets, dress pants, and dress shoes for men (ties are optional); dresses, suits, blouses, and dress pants for women. Please leave the jeans, shorts, tank tops, yoga pants, sandals, flip-flops, Crocs™, and sneakers in your stateroom. Jackets are optional for brunch.

What to Wear for Dinner
Generally speaking, "cruise casual" is the way to go in all spots except for Palo and Remy: collared shirts, blouses, cotton pants, jeans, and sundresses are generally acceptable for evenings

in all other restaurants—shorts, swimsuits, T-shirts, and tank tops are not. On select nights, there will be a theme: tropical, pirate attire, semi-formal, etc. On such days, the desired style of dress will be noted in the *Personal Navigator*. (While parents are the best judges of what attire is appropriate for their children, most guests over the age of 13 are usually comfortable wearing attire that is similar to what is recommended for all passengers.) Note that Palo and Remy, grown-ups-only destinations, are considered more formal and guests are asked to dress accordingly: pants and shirt are required for men (jacket optional at Palo, required for Remy), and a dress or pants and shirt combo for women. No jeans, shorts, flip-flops, or sneakers, please. Likewise, the indoor area of Meridian Bar, located between Palo and Remy, has the same formal dress code as Palo. However, the outdoor patio of Meridian has a slightly more casual vibe (think business casual).

Wine and Dine

Each of the table-service restaurants (except for Remy) offers many vintages by the glass or by the bottle. If you order a bottle and fail to finish it by meal's end, ask your server to store it for you. (You'll get it with the next evening's meal.)

For guests who expect to enjoy more than one bottle of wine over the course of the cruise, Disney offers two wine packages (with red and white selections).

Special Dietary Needs

Certain special dietary needs may be met aboard Disney cruise ships. All requests should be made well in advance, preferably at the time of booking the cruise package. It's always a good idea to confirm the request prior to setting sail.

HOT TIP

Children's menus are available in all shipboard restaurants (with the obvious exceptions of Palo and Remy). Buffets all stock kid-friendly vittles such as mac and cheese and chicken tenders.

SELF-SERVE, FAST FOOD, AND SNACKS

Vibe

This teens-only spot—which can be found on all ships—serves up fruit smoothies and other soft drinks. There are lots of games and magazines, and some refreshments are free of charge. However, there is an extra charge for smoothies. This area is hopping all day—and often past midnight. FYI: The teen spots on the *Magic* and *Wonder* used to be known as Aloft and The Stack, respectively.

Beverage Station

There is a self-serve station on every ship. On the *Magic* and *Wonder*, you'll find it on Deck 9, aft (port side). On the *Dream* and *Fantasy*, look for the beverage station on Deck 11, midship (there is a station on each side of the Mickey pool). Help yourself to water, juice, soda, iced tea, lemonade, coffee, hot chocolate, and hot tea. There is an ice machine, too. The station is generally open 24 hours a day, though not all selections are available at all times. (If the machine fails to dispense ice, get some via room service delivery.) Soft drinks are free here and with meals, but not at bars or through room service.

Cabanas

Located on the *Dream*, *Fantasy*, and *Magic*, this indoor casual eatery serves three meals a day. This spot recalls a breezy boardwalk along the Pacific coast, with a dash of Disney (i.e., colorful *Nemo*-themed mosaics). Made-to-order breakfast and lunch selections are offered "on the boardwalk" on most days (check your *Personal Navigator* for times and specifics). In other words, a variety of food stations proffer freshly prepared edibles. Dinner is a table-service affair. Cocktails may be ordered from the Clam Bar. Cabanas is located on Deck 11, aft on the *Dream* and *Fantasy*, Deck 9 aft on the *Magic*.

Cove Cafe

A cozy, adults-only lounge, Cove Cafe can be found aboard all ships. It features espresso and other specialty coffees, and a full bar (fees apply). Complimentary cakes and cookies are available, too. Books and magazines are on hand for on-site perusing, as is a TV (often showing a big game or the news). Board games may be borrowed, too. Wireless Internet access is available (for a fee). The cafe is near the Quiet Cove pool.

Eye Scream and Frozone Treats

Dream and *Fantasy*: Guests craving a chilly treat can find satisfaction at adjoining snack stations. Eye Scream (with theming inspired by famous eyeball Mike Wazowski) doles out soft-serve ice creams. Mike's neighbor, a spot that pays tribute to Frozone from *The Incredibles*, serves made-to-order mixed fruit smoothies and cocktails (for a fee).

Flo's Cafe

Dream and *Fantasy*: Flo's Cafe, located on Deck 11 near the Donald pool, is actually a trio of side-by-side walk-up windows, all themed to characters from the animated feature *Cars*. Here you'll find Luigi's Pizza, Tow Mater's Grill,

and Fillmore's Favorites. Menu options at these filling stations include pizza (often featuring a special pizza of the day), chicken tenders, salads, sandwich wraps, fruit, burgers, and more. Luigi's tends to stay open the latest of the three.

Pinocchio's Pizzeria

Magic and *Wonder*: This counter-service spot serves spirits and soft drinks (for a fee), and cheese and pepperoni pizzas (no charge for food). There is often a special pizza of the day. Be sure to ask.

Pluto's Dog House

Magic and *Wonder*: Located on Deck 9, aft, this counter

97

service spot serves hot dogs, bratwurst, burgers, veggie burgers, fish burgers, grilled chicken sandwiches, tacos, and chicken tenders.

Goofy's Galley

Magic and *Wonder*: A popular spot for a snack or a light meal, this counter features self-serve soft-serve ice cream. It also offers salads, wraps, pressed panini sandwiches, cookies, and fresh fruit.

Topsider Buffet

Located on the *Disney Wonder*, this self-service buffet offers breakfast and lunch. The morning meal brings selections such as fresh fruit, cereal, eggs, sausage, oatmeal, etc. Lunch fare

usually has a theme: Italian, Chinese, seafood, etc. (Check a *Personal Navigator*, or at the eatery itself, to learn if there's a theme for the meal.) In addition to the buffet (which you will encounter as you enter), there is a serving station by the seating area. This area usually serves omelets in the morning and something special for lunch. There are indoor tables and others out on the deck. Topsider offers table service and casual dining for dinner on most evenings.

ROOM SERVICE

Stateroom dining service delivers 24 hours a day—very handy if you're traveling with children or if you have a serious snack craving in between meals. Most menu items are included with your cruise package. At press time, selections included soups, salads, sandwiches, burgers, pizza, cookies, and selections for kids. There is a charge for beverages and some snack selections (such as candy, popcorn, wine, beer, soda, and bottled water). Gratuity is not always included.

SPECIAL DINING EXPERIENCES
Pirates IN the Caribbean Party

If there's one thing Disney really knows how to do right, it's throw a party. On one night during most cruises, guests enjoy a buccaneering soirée. If you own any pirate attire or regalia, wear it to the big event. (You may purchase some from a ship shop, too.) It takes place on the upper decks, where pirate villains set their sights on taking over the ship. An epic battle ensues as the good guys take on the villains. The greatest spectacle of all is the show's grand finale—fireworks (offered on most itineraries). It's the only display of its kind done at sea. A feast fit for a pirate king is served post pyrotechnics (in Topsider on the *Wonder,* and in Cabanas on the *Magic, Dream,* and *Fantasy.*

FUN FOOD FACTS

Apparently, cruising makes passengers exceptionally hungry. Here's what's put away on an average 7-night voyage on the *Disney Magic*:

- Rib-eye steak—800 to 1,000 pounds
- Beef strip loin—2,000 pounds
- Beef tenderloin—2,500 pounds
- Whole chickens—9,000 pounds
- Fresh salmon—900 pounds
- Grouper—300 pounds
- Shrimp—2,200 pounds
- Lobster tail—900 pounds
- Fresh melon—10,500 pounds
- Fresh pineapple—4,400 pounds
- Yogurt—2,400 tubs
- Cereal—7,920 packets
- Individual eggs—44,500
- Tomato ketchup—26,000 packets
- Mayonnaise—15,000 packets
- Sugar—40,000 packets
- Beer—7,400 bottles/cans
- Wine and champagne—2,200 bottles

HOT TIP

Adults may bring their own (unopened) bottle of wine to dinner. A $20 corking fee will be charged to your shipboard account for each bottle that was not purchased on board.

Character Breakfast

An up-close-and-personal morning starring furry favorites is a very Disney way to start the day. (This is available for most itineraries on the *Magic* and *Wonder*.) Everyone may attend one character-hosted breakfast per cruise. Check your Dining Ticket for assigned morning and location (characters vary). Characters have even been known to dance with guests. Don't forget your camera!

Many of the character breakfast selections remain staples—eggs, bacon, cereal, fruit, yogurt, and French toast, for example.

Captain's Gala Dinner

Even on this, one of the planet's most casual of cruises, there is a chance to don your finery and join the sparkle and glitter of this black-tie (optional) affair. If you'd rather not get completely decked out, go with a business casual look (but not too casual). The French-continental menu is offered in each of the main dining rooms on all ships. A menu favorite is the baked lobster tail served in the shell with lemon butter and rice. The Captain's Gala is offered on most cruises of 7 nights or longer. It is often preceded by a reception in the lobby.

Farewell Dinner

Presented on the final evening of cruises 7 nights or longer, this evening meal is a chance to enjoy favorite dishes, celebrate new friends, and perhaps start planning (or at least dreaming about) your next cruise.

Family Tea

A tea party with one of Disney's beloved characters is a true kid-pleaser. During this break in the day's activities, the party's host will tell stories, sign autographs, and pose for pictures. The tea is offered on most cruises of 7 nights or longer on the *Magic* and *Wonder*. Reservations may be made at Guest Services. (There is no extra charge for Family Tea, but a reservation is necessary.)

Bars and Lounges

From elegant spots with live piano music to rousing sports bars, Disney ships have a bounty of bars and lounges in which to wet your whistle or simply unwind and watch the waves or the sunset. (Most beverages offered in these spots come with an extra charge.)

Bon Voyage

A casual lounge located on Deck 3, midship (*Dream* and *Fantasy*). Beverages are available all day.

Cadillac Lounge

Unique to the Route 66 entertainment zone (*Wonder*), this sophisticated spot celebrates classic cars with soothing music, wine, martinis, and other drinks.

Cove Cafe

This cozy adults-only lounge can be found aboard all of the ships in Disney's fleet. It offers specialty coffees, and a full bar (charges apply). Complimentary snacks are available, too. Magazines are on hand for on-site perusing, as is a TV. Board games may also be borrowed for on-site use. Wireless Internet is available (for a fee).

Currents

A breezy spot with stellar ocean views, Currents is on Deck 13, forward (*Dream* and *Fantasy*).

District Lounge

This intimate bar is located in the *Dream*'s District entertainment zone.

Dance Club

A butterfly-themed hot spot, Evolution celebrates all styles of music on the *Dream*. On the *Fantasy*, it's The Tube, a dance spot that pays tribute to the city of London. The venues feature various activities and dance parties. (Guests must be at least 18 years old to come here at night, 21 to imbibe.)

Fathoms

This After Hours joint (*Magic*) fancies itself a celebration of the sea. It uses special effects, lighting, and sound to create different atmospheres from early evening to late night. There's a dance floor, plus tables and bar seating. Themed parties are thrown here on select evenings.

Keys

The *Magic*'s re-imagined piano bar, this lounge serves cocktails and wines by the glass. Keys provides a lovely, musical retreat.

La Piazza

The *Fantasy*'s celebration of Italian cities features a festive carousel bar. Venetian masks and glasswork add to the atmosphere.

Meridian Bar

Found on the *Dream* and *Fantasy*, Meridian is located on Deck 12, aft, and has indoor and outdoor seating. The dress code for the indoor area: Dress pants and shirt are required for men and a dress or dress pants for women. On the outside deck, the dress code is cruise casual (jeans and shorts are okay, swimsuits and tank tops are not).

Ooh La La

A *Fantasy* champagne bar, this space was inspired by a French boudoir.

Outlook Café

Overlooking the Quiet Cove Pool on the *Wonder* (above Cove Cafe), this lounge serves cocktails and coffee drinks.

Pink

An elegant nightspot designed to look like the inside of a champagne bottle, this festive lounge is in the District entertainment zone on the *Dream*.

Promenade Lounge

This lounge serves cocktails and soft drinks on the *Magic* and *Wonder*. At night, it offers live music.

Signals

Located on Deck 9 of the *Magic* and *Wonder*, this poolside spot serves cocktails and soft drinks.

Skyline

The *Dream*'s District area and the *Fantasy*'s Europa boast Skyline, a cosmopolitan bar with majestic views of famous cities from around the world. The cityscapes change over the course of the evening.

(continued on page 106)

BE BORED: WE DARE YOU!

On any given day, guests aboard a Disney ship have a plethora of activities to engage in. On one of our sea days, we were offered the following:

10 A.M. Yoga

11 A.M. Pool Games

11:30 A.M. Meet Disney Character Friends

1 P.M. Disney Behind the Scenes (guest speaker)

1:30 P.M. Princess Gathering

1:30 P.M. Chip It Golf

2 P.M. Funnel Vision Movie

2 P.M. Disney's Anyone Can Cook Series

2 P.M. Beer Tasting

2:30 P.M. Wine Tasting

2:45 P.M. Art of the Theme Show (ship tour)

3 P.M. Pool Games

3:30 P.M. Jack Jack's Incredible Diaper Dash

3:30 P.M. Jackpot Bingo

4:30 P.M. Cruisin' for Trivia

4:30–5:30 P.M. Pirates Life for Me Game Show

4:45–5:30 P.M. Salsa Dancing

5:30–6:15 P.M. Dance Music

5:30 P.M. Family Dance Party

5:45–6:30 P.M. Captain's Welcome Reception

5:45–6:30 P.M. Family Dance Party

6:15 P.M. Villains Tonight!

7:30–8:30 P.M. Family Game Shows
(Mickey Mania)

7:30–8:30 P.M. Pin Trading

7:45–8:30 P.M. Captain's Welcome Reception

8:30 P.M. Tailgate Party

8:30 P.M. Villains Tonight!

9:30–10:15 P.M. Who Wants to Be a Mouseketeer?

10:15–11:30 P.M. Family Karaoke

10:15 P.M. Cabaret Show

10:45 P.M. Disco Legends Party

12–2 A.M. Dance Party

Note that some events are repeated to accommodate guests with different dining times. Some activities are for grown-ups only. These listings were taken from actual *Personal Navigators*.

Sports Bar

A sports fan's dream come true, this lounge has a satellite feed, plus suds and wings, hot dogs, or other munchies. It's Diversions on the *Wonder*, 687 on the *Dream*, and O'Gill's on the *Fantasy* and *Magic*.

The Tube

Housed in the *Fantasy*'s Europa district, The Tube is a metropolitan dance club themed to the London Underground (aka the tube).

Vista Café

Dream and *Fantasy* guests in need of a java jolt can head to this cheery destination on Deck 4, midship. Snacks and cocktails are served, too.

WaveBands

Vintage radios and album covers line the walls and set the stage for a lively dance club. A deejay keeps the place grooving till the wee hours. All manner of drinks are available at this Route 66 club (*Wonder*).

Waves

An open-air bar on the *Dream* and the *Fantasy*, this spot serves beverages all day.

Entertainment

For some, a deck chair, a good book, and a steady stream of sunshine are all the entertainment required. Others may delight in an evening of dancing or a bingo-filled afternoon. And some are satisfied with nothing short of an all-out Broadway-style stage show. Fortunately, Disney Cruise Line has all of the above, plus guest lecturers, tours, and more. Check the daily *Personal Navigator* for show schedules. Note that all shows are not presented every day or on every cruise. The entertainment lineup is tweaked from time to time,

so some details may differ during your cruise.

STAGE SHOWS

The majestic Walt Disney Theatre (Deck 4, forward, on the *Magic* and *Wonder*; Decks 3 and 4, forward, on the *Dream* and *Fantasy*) is the venue in which Disney Cruise Line presents lavish musical performances.

The auditorium also hosts variety shows, the big-payoff final bingo game, and more.

The Golden Mickeys

A dynamic production that pays tribute to the musical legacy of Walt Disney Studios. It's got all the glitz and glamour of a Hollywood celebration, paying homage to the comedy, romance, and heroes (plus a few key villains) of classic Disney animated films. This show is presented on the *Wonder* and *Dream*. It's a crowd-pleaser (and worthy of a Golden Mickey)!

Welcome Aboard Show

This sweet presentation is a nice way to "meet" your ship's crew. The captain, cruise director, and many of their comrades introduce themselves and welcome guests aboard. Musical numbers and vaudeville-like variety acts round out the bill. This show is presented on cruises of 7 nights and longer.

Disney's Aladdin—A Musical Spectacular

This musical showcases a variety of classic (and new!) songs and characters from the animated feature and regales guests with theatrical treats. It's a *Fantasy* exclusive.

Disney's Believe

Who doesn't believe in the power of pixie dust? A little girl named Sophia certainly does. But her serious-minded father, Mr. Greenaway, is a much tougher sell. Follow his journey from skeptic to believer in this rousing musical show. In addition to classic Disney tunes, this crowd-pleaser features the lovely original song "What Makes a Garden Grow." It is presented on the *Dream* and *Fantasy*.

Disney Dreams—An Enchanted Classic

This bedtime story features a galaxy of familiar Disney stars, including the Blue Fairy, Peter Pan, Belle, Beast, Aladdin, Cinderella, and Ariel. Together and through the power of song and dance, the characters teach a skeptical girl about the power of dreams. It takes place on the *Magic* and *Wonder*.

Toy Story—The Musical

Fans of the beloved movie will be pleased to see it come to life in one of the largest productions ever developed for a cruise ship. The story isn't entirely new—but much of the music is. The tunes help tell the story of Buzz, Woody, and the toys from Andy's room in an ambitious way. This show is presented exclusively on the *Wonder*.

Twice Charmed—An Original Twist on the Cinderella Story

A Broadway-style extravaganza (*Magic* only), this musical production begins with the wedding of Cinderella and Prince Charming. Things take a sudden turn when the wicked Fairy Godfather makes his presence known and, after granting a wish to one evil stepmother, sends the family back in time, where—*gasp*—the glass slipper gets broken! Does this turn of events destroy

Cinderella's chances of living happily ever after? You'll just have to catch the show to find out.

Villains Tonight!

It seems old Hades is losing his evil edge and, with it, his status as "Lord of the Underworld." Perish the thought! In an effort to regain his meanie mojo, he enlists some of Disney's most dastardly villains in what turns out to be an enjoyable comic/musical revue. The hour-long show can be seen on the *Magic* and *Dream*.

Disney's Wishes

As high school kids face graduation day, they discover that the secret to becoming a grown-up is to stay connected to your inner child. And what's a wonderful way to do that? By making a wish and spending a fun-filled, musical—and magical—day at Disneyland. This show is presented on the *Fantasy*.

Remember the Magic: Farewell Show

This show wraps up the trip as performers celebrate a week of shipboard activities and island-hopping. This particular production is presented on the *Magic* and *Wonder*, but the *Fantasy* and *Dream* have special good-bye shows, too.

DECK PARTIES

When it comes to on-deck celebrations, the area by the family pool (Goofy's or Donald's, depending on the ship) is party central. Starting with a Sailing Away Celebration and continuing with daily dance fests with Disney characters, live bands, and fireworks (except for Alaska itineraries), it seems like there is always a reason to party. Check the daily *Personal Navigator* for celebration specifics.

109

FAMILY ENTERTAINMENT
D Lounge

This family-friendly lounge and nightclub is on the *Magic*, *Dream*, and *Fantasy* (Deck 4, midship). Head here for dance parties, character greetings, karaoke, games, and more.

Studio Sea

A colorful "TV studio" environment (on the *Wonder*) is the setting for audience-participation family game shows. *Mickey Mania* lets you put your knowledge of Disney trivia to the test, while Karaoke Night encourages families to take the stage and sing together. Finally, the Family Dance Party gives everyone a chance to kick up their heels (or sneakers) and enjoy a party for guests of all ages. Keep in mind that the entertainment lineup, though always dynamic, is subject to change from time to time.

Character Breakfast

On most cruises that are 7 nights or longer (on the *Magic* and *Wonder*), a bountiful breakfast is hosted by Disney friends.

Family Tea

Guests of all ages, but especially younger ones (on 7-night-or-longer cruises on the *Magic* and *Wonder*), are invited to enjoy afternoon tea with some of their favorite Disney friends. The event takes place at Studio Sea (*Wonder*) and D Lounge (*Magic*). In addition to learning the proper way to serve tea and cookies, guests are treated to stories about their host's or hostess's adventures. Tickets are necessary and are available at Guest Services (they're free). For details, turn to page 101.

FOR GROWN-UPS ONLY

The 18-and-over set on the *Magic* and *Wonder* can attend demonstrations (i.e., Disney's Art of Entertaining), lectures and conversations with guest speakers, tours, and specially tailored nighttime events (such as *Match Your Mate*, a game show in which you and your mate will find out how much you know about each other), as well as theme nights, cabaret shows, and much more.

On the *Dream* and *Fantasy*, adults have the chance to participate in interactive cooking demonstrations as part of the Anyone Can Cook! series; learn the secrets of Disney animation in the Illusion of Life series; and attend a presentation about the making of the ship.

JUST FOR KIDS

The wildly popular kids' programs and activities tend to elicit raves from participants and parents alike. For starters, adults who leave their kids at supervised facilities can be assured that the watch-word here is safety. There are plenty of counselors on hand, and the secured programming ensures that they know where every child is at any given time. Kids are checked in with Youth Activities when entering and signed out when exiting with an authorized guardian. Upon check-in, each child is given an electronic wristband. (The

DID YOU KNOW?

The anchor on the *Disney Magic* weighs 28,200 pounds— about the same as three full-grown elephants!

band assists with the check-in and check-out process and adds an additional level of security to youth venues.) Records of a child's allergies or other particular needs are entered into their file.

Every child is required to wear a wristband that identifies him or her as a participant in the program. Parents have Wave Phones (which can be found in all staterooms) and can be contacted immediately if their child has a problem or just wants to see them.

Cleanliness is a priority, too. In fact, kids entering the Oceaneer Club and Lab are promptly asked to wash their hands. Play areas are cleaned three times a day, with a deep-down cleansing done at the end of each day.

The children's programs are concentrated on Deck 5, and kids registered into the secured programming always remain in either the Lab or Club. The specially tailored programming is open to kids who are completely potty-trained, able to interact comfortably within the counselor-to-child ratio groups, and able to mix well with peers.

Kids between ages 3 and 12 can choose to play in the Oceaneer Club or Oceaneer Lab based on whatever interests them. Siblings and friends between the ages of 3 and 12 can play together regardless, as kids are not segregated by age group. And don't worry about little ones ever being dominated by bigger kids—participants are closely monitored at all times.

Kids who exhibit any symptoms of illness—even if it's just a runny nose—will not be allowed to participate. If a child becomes disruptive, he or she may not be allowed to participate without a parent or guardian present.

Except for the nursery, there is no fee for youth

ages 3–12 (potty-trained) on all Disney ships.

At the Oceaneer Club, kids will find a combination of free play and structured activities featuring interactive, playful experiences with some of their favorite Disney characters. These may include dancing with Snow White, reading a story with Belle, learning how to be a pirate from Captain Hook, and even playing games with Mickey Mouse. Lunch and dinner are served (at no extra charge). It's open from 9 A.M. till midnight.

activities. The following descriptions of the youth activities were accurate at press time, but specifics are subject to change from time to time.

Oceaneer Club

A wonderfully detailed adventure zone, this club has several distinctly themed areas on the *Magic*, *Dream*, and *Fantasy* and a pirate theme on the *Wonder*. In addition to computer games, costumes, and other games, there are many organized activities. It's open to kids

HOT TIP

Looking for a little privacy on the *Magic* or *Wonder*? There is a little-known outdoor nook—complete with comfy chairs—on Deck 7, aft.

113

Oceaneer Lab

The Oceaneer Lab is open to (potty-trained) kids ages 3–12 on all Disney ships. It is located on Deck 5, midship. The futuristic space is filled with wacky inventions and opportunities for exploration. There are games, books, toys, child-friendly computers, video games, drawing materials, and more. As with the Oceaneer Club, there are also several imaginative organized activities. It is open from 9 A.M. till midnight.

Programs here allow kids to be very hands-on while learning the skills of Disney animators, becoming a sleuth to solve mysteries with Disney characters, and joining a chef for a *Ratatouille*-inspired cooking experience. Check a *Personal Navigator* for specific dates and times for various activities while on board. Lunch and dinner are served (at no additional charge).

Reminder: *Kids ages 8–12 may check themselves in and out of the Oceaneer Lab with their parents' permission.*

Edge

On the *Magic*, kids ages 11–14 (tweens) can play captain as they steer the ship from a scaled replica of the bridge. LCD screens provide a simulated view from the ship's actual bridge. There are video games, arts and crafts, and flat-panel TVs for movie-viewing as well. There are evening activities such as scavenger hunts and karaoke, too. The *Wonder*'s Edge is similar, but doesn't have a bridge replica. Edge can be found on Deck 2 on the *Magic* and *Wonder*.

Also a tween space on the *Dream* and *Fantasy*, Edge is located on Deck 13 inside the forward funnel. Its high-tech features include an illuminated dance floor, a video wall, and notebook computers for game-playing.

HOT TIP

If your little one isn't completely potty-trained, Flounder's Reef or It's a Small World Nursery is the place to go for supervised activities and babysitting. Keep in mind that there is an hourly fee to use the ship's nursery.

Flounder's Reef Nursery and It's a Small World Nursery

Open to children ages 12 weeks through 3 years, these colorful spaces are the ships' babysitting centers. (Flounder's Reef is on the *Wonder*, while It's a Small World is on the *Magic*, *Dream*, and *Fantasy*.) For an hourly fee, the nursery offers toddler-friendly activities and a quiet area, complete with cribs.

No food is available at the nursery, but if parents provide prepared bottles or jarred food that is clearly labeled with a child's name, staffers will happily feed their hungry tyke. Space is limited and gets booked early. In fact, reservations are accepted via *www.disneycruise.com* and on embarkation day on a first-come, first-served basis. Due to the high demand, multiple requests might not be honored—so don't count on securing several sessions, though it can't hurt to try. The fee for the babysitting service is $6 per hour for the first child, $5 per each additional child with a one-hour minimum (only siblings net the discount). The ships' nurseries are generally open from 9 A.M. until 11 P.M. *In-stateroom babysitting is not available on any ship.*

TEENS ONLY

Teens can enjoy their own special hangout and activities while aboard Disney ships. Vibe is their exclusive place to hang out. (If you're old enough to vote, KEEP OUT!) It's got popular music, games, dance parties, big-screen TVs, and more.

The activities and sodas are free, but smoothies cost extra. Other teen-oriented programs include karaoke, organized sports activities, a pool party, and more. Vibe is open from 11 A.M. till 2 A.M.

FUN AND GAMES
Arcade
Located on Deck 9 of the *Magic* and *Wonder* by Goofy's Family Pool, Quarter Masters Arcade is a small room replete with modern electronic games and an air hockey table. On the *Dream* and *Fantasy*, the pirate-themed—and appropriately named— Arr-cade can be found on Deck 11. You will have to purchase credits to play in any of the ships' arcades.

Bingo
Perhaps it's something in the ocean air, but nothing brings out the bingo fanatic in you like a few days at sea. The closest thing to gambling that you'll find on a Disney vessel, the daily bingo sessions are extremely popular.

You have to be at least 18 to play, but kids can watch over a grown-up's shoulder and cheer them on. Each bingo session has several individual games. Cards can be purchased one at a time or in family packages. You can even play along electronically—a neat technological twist that allows you to watch several cards at once. There is a rolling jackpot—meaning that if no one wins the big prize one day, it rolls over to the next session. That is until the last day bingo is played. Then they call numbers until somebody wins. (On a recent cruise, a very lucky guest won a $7,000 jackpot. Sadly, it wasn't us. There's always next cruise!)

Games
Ping-pong, foosball, shuffleboard, basketball . . .

they're all here. Equipment can usually be found by the tables or courts. (Don't monopolize it—it's for everyone to share.) Kooky competitions are sometimes held poolside. The *Dream* and *Fantasy* offer mini-golf and sports simulators (there is a charge to use the simulators). See a *Personal Navigator* for details.

Movies

The Buena Vista Theatre shows new film releases—some in 3-D (courtesy of Disney's patented technology). This is the perfect place to head when the weather is less than ideal. Get there early, as the seats fill up quickly.

If you prefer your flicks alfresco, make a beeline for the Goofy or Donald pool. A jumbo screen (on the forward funnel and known as Funnel Vision) broadcasts Disney features, sports, and more throughout the cruise.

SHOPPING

While on board Disney's cruise ships, you can enjoy tax-free (on all items) and duty-free (select items) shopping. Check the *Personal Navigator* for hours and details about special merchandise events such as pin trading or Captain's Signing (when the captain autographs collectibles that can be purchased on board).

HOT TIP

When the weather's good, it's breezy on deck. When the weather's less than perfect, it is breezier. When the weather's bad, it's downright gusty. If you've got long hair and you intend to explore outside deck areas, bring a band or a clip to tie your hair back.

The shops have limited hours due to U.S. Customs regulations and can't operate during any time when the ship is in port. Use your stateroom key (Key to the World) to buy items in the ship's shops and on Castaway Cay. Purchases will be charged to your stateroom account. (The island's post office accepts cash only.)

Onboard Shops
Preludes (All ships)
There is a well-stocked snack bar/concessions window on either side of the Walt Disney Theatre. It closes at about 10 P.M. but opens at different times. Among the items for sale are cookies, candies, nuts, and drinks (spirits and soft drinks are served for a fee, too).

Mickey's Mainsail
(Dream and Fantasy)
Located on Deck 3, midship, Mickey stocks all manner of Disney and Disney Cruise Line merchandise.

Mickey's Mates
(Magic and Wonder)
Located on Deck 4, forward, this shop offers Disney Cruise Line logo merchandise, including souvenirs, clothing, beach towels, swimwear, mugs, character costumes, postcards, and plush toys.

Sea Treasures
(Dream and Fantasy)
Located on Deck 3, midship, the treasures here include collectibles, sportswear, swimwear, purses, watches, fragrances, and accessories.

Treasure Ketch
(Magic and Wonder)
Directly across the hall from Mickey's Mates on Deck 4, this shop sells jewelry, loose

gemstones, and limited-edition Disney collectibles. There's a selection of clothing, including shirts, sweatshirts, hats, jackets, and other Disney Cruise Line logo items. The store also stocks batteries, postcards, disposable cameras, books, magazines, sun-care products, and a limited selection of sundries (including aspirin and Dramamine). Be sure to check out the nightly promotions—there is a new one each evening.

Up Beat and Radar Trap
(Magic and Wonder)
Located on Deck 3, forward, these counter-service spots offer tax- and duty-free liquor, snacks, and more. Note that any liquor purchased here may not be consumed while on board. It will be delivered to your room on the last evening of your cruise. Everything else may be consumed (or worn) during the cruise.

Whitecaps
(Dream and Fantasy)
Found on Deck 3, forward, this is the place for duty-free items such as perfume, watches, liquor, and tobacco products (which will be delivered to your room on the last night of your cruise).

Whozits & Whatzits
(Dream and Fantasy)
A tiny shop located on Deck 11, near the Donald pool, Whozits & Whatzits sells deckwear, magazines, sunscreen, towels, and other poolside necessities.

SHOPS ON CASTAWAY CAY
Buy the Seashore
This shop offers island-themed souvenirs such as hats, totes, and shirts, plus beach toys, towels, and drinkware. Also available are sun-care products and camera supplies.

DUTY-FREE SHOPPING—RULES TO SHOP BY

If unlimited duty (tax)-free shopping sounds too good to be true, well, it is. There are limits. Federally enforced limits. Specifics vary slightly, depending on where you do your shopping. Know that the rules are mandated by U.S. law and are subject to change.

Bahamas—Each guest re-entering the U.S. from the Bahamas can bring up to $800 (U.S. currency) worth of duty-free treasures. Those of legal drinking age (that's 21 and up) can pick up two liters of alcohol, of which one must be produced in a CBERA country and purchased in the Bahamas. Legal adults (18 and over) are limited to 200 cigarettes and 100 cigars (with the exception of Cuban cigars—they're illegal to bring into the U.S.).

Eastern Caribbean—Guests who voyage to the Eastern Caribbean and back to the U.S. can bring back up to $1,600 worth of duty-free stuff. However, no more than $800 of it can be purchased on the ship, St. Maarten, San Juan, and Castaway Cay combined. The rest has to come from St. Thomas. Or, the entire $1,600 may be used toward purchases made on St. Thomas alone. Got that? If not, read it again—it's important. As for alcohol, each legal drinker is limited to five liters—only one liter can come from St. Maarten, San Juan, or the ship, with an additional four liters being exempt if they were purchased on St. Thomas and at least one liter of that allotment was produced in the U.S. Virgin Islands.

Each guest 18 or older is limited to five cartons of cigarettes (only one carton may be purchased on St. Maarten, San Juan, or on the ship, with an additional four cartons being exempt if purchased on St. Thomas). You're allowed 100 cigars (no Cubans).

Western Caribbean—If you are returning from the Western Caribbean to the U.S., you may bring up to $800 worth of duty-free booty from the ports of call on your itinerary. If you're at least 21 years old, you can buy one liter of alcohol. Older than 18? You're entitled to 200 cigarettes and 100 cigars (again, Cuban cigars are not permitted).

GAME ON!

Heads up, sports fans. There is a dedicated sports pub on each of the Disney cruise ships. The laid-back location is Diversions on the *Wonder*, 687 on the *Dream*, and O'Gill's on the *Fantasy* and *Magic*. It's a TV-filled room with a multitude of live events being broadcast at any time. There's often a mini-buffet available (think wings or hot dogs) and plenty of suds to wash down the snacks. (Snacks are free, but all beverages are extra.) If there's a particular game you're interested in, ask about it at the door. This spot is ideal for watching football, with up to six games shown at a time. Baseball is also a popular draw, as is pro basketball. The occasional hockey match-up is shown, too. We love it here!

She Sells Seashells and Everything Else

Have to have a Castaway Cay hat, pin, or T-shirt? This is the place to get it. A mini-bazaar comprised of a hut or two and outdoor stands, "She" also sells beach toys, towels, batteries, sun-care products, tropical clothing, and, of course, collectible pins and plush toys. You will also find postcards, beachwear, beach toys, hats, and a whole lot more.

SPORTS AND RECREATION
Fitness Center

The fitness center is located within the Vista Spa & Salon on the *Wonder* and within the Senses Spa & Salon on the *Magic*, *Dream*, and *Fantasy*. There is no fee to use the equipment, which includes treadmills, bikes, stair-climbing machines, free weights, and more. (Some of the equipment sport TVs—bring headphones or borrow a pair at the front desk.) Fitness consultations are offered. The fitness center is open from about 6 A.M. to 10 P.M., while the spa is open from 8 A.M. to 8 P.M.

Wide World of Sports Deck
(Magic and Wonder)

Deck 10 is home to the Wide World of Sports deck. Though open to everyone, it's a huge kid and teen magnet. The basketball hoops are hopping day and night. Basketballs and other equipment are on-site (no charge). This deck is also popular with casual strollers, though jogging on the *Magic* and *Wonder* is relegated to Deck 4 (where one lap is about one-third of a mile). Deck 4 is where you'll find the shuffleboard court, too.

Goofy's Sports Deck
(Dream and Fantasy)

Located on Deck 13, aft, the always bustling Goofy's Sports Deck is an all-ages, open-air activity center. The basketball court can easily be converted to a volleyball court or a small soccer arena. The zone also has a sports simulator (soccer, golf, tennis, and basketball; fees apply)

NOW IT'S TIME . . .

. . . to say good-bye. At the end of a cruise on the *Magic* or *Wonder*, kids who participated in children's programs can take part in a good-bye celebration known as Friendship Rocks! Presented at the Walt Disney Theatre, the musical celebration is quite popular—even Mickey and Minnie join in the festivities—so arrive early for a good seat. Note that all pint-sized participants receive a souvenir T-shirt to mark the occasion.

and an honest-to-goodness (or is that Goof-ness?) mini golf course (designed by Goofy and his son, Max).

Swimming
(Magic and Wonder)

There are three guest swimming areas on board, all located on Deck 9: Mickey's Pool (*Wonder* kids' pool) and Aqualab (*Magic*) are located toward the back, or aft; Goofy's Family Pool is midship; and the Quiet Cove Adult Pool is on Deck 9, forward. Though the names are self-explanatory, we'll state the obvious: Mickey's pool is for the young'uns and their friends. The Quiet Cove pool is earmarked for splashers ages 18 and up. Don't let the name fool you; Quiet Cove may be for grown-ups, but it isn't always the picture of serenity. Organized games engage giddy adults from time to time. Finally, Goofy's pool is for everyone, but kids under age 10 must be accompanied by an adult, and swimmers must be potty-trained. Goofy's pool and Quiet Cove

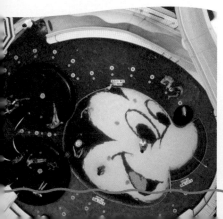

have two whirlpools each. Mickey's pool, which is in the shape of the Big Cheese's head, has a special element: Mickey's Splash Zone. The soft-surface spray area is reserved for tots wearing swim diapers.

AquaDunk
(Magic)

Step into the 3-story, trans-luscent tube, the trapdoor opens and . . . kerplunk! The cool ride is quick and splashy. Guests must be at least 48 inches tall to take the plunge.

AquaLab
(Magic)

Deck 9, aft, is home to the *Magic*'s new "splashtacular" squirt zone: AquaLab. This interactive playground is open to guests age 3 and up. Families may frolic among pop jets, bubblers, and geysers, and slip along the "Twist and Spout" waterslide. (Guests must be between 38 and 84 inches tall to ride.)

123

Swimming
(Dream and Fantasy)

Deck 11 is pool central on these ships. Donald's Pool is the family pool and can be found midship. Mickey's Pool is strictly for kids and their guardians, and the Quiet Cove pool is a grown-ups-only splash zone. Nemo's Reef is a soft-surface spray zone for the toddler set (swim diapers are required).

Tired of all that poolside relaxation? Head for Deck 12 and the ship's ultimate adrenaline-inducer: the AquaDuck. This 765-foot-long "water coaster" propels guests through a clear tube on a journey that includes a trip over the ocean and through the forward funnel, and a 4-deck drop. Check a *Personal Navigator* for operating hours. Guests must be at least 42 inches tall to

ride the AquaDuck and 54 inches tall to ride alone. Kids under age 7 must be accompanied by someone 14 years of age or older. It's a hoot—and not as scary as it looks!

AquaLab
(Fantasy and Magic)

Deck 12, aft, is home to the *Fantasy's* colorful family splash zone called AquaLab. You'll find it on Deck 9, aft, on the *Magic*.

Satellite Falls
(Fantasy)

A watery haven for grown-ups, this Deck 13, forward, spot has a circular splash pool with benches and a cascading curtain of water.

Spa & Salon
(All ships)

Pampering, Disney style, can be enjoyed at the ships' ocean-view spas and salons —Vista Spa & Salon on the *Wonder* and Senses Spa &

Salon on the *Magic*, *Dream* and *Fantasy*. Here, fitness-minded folk can work with a trainer, take a class, or work out solo. As for the pampering, well, that can come by way of any number of treatments.

Book appointments ahead of time by visiting *www.disneycruise.com*, or go to the spa when you board the ship. The spa and salon are open to guests ages 18 and older.

The spa is open from 8 A.M. to 8 P.M. every day, *except* on days when the ship is docked at its home port. Prices are posted in the spa. If you miss a reserved treatment, your stateroom will be charged. Note that Cabana Massages (located at Serenity Bay on Castaway Cay) and the Vista Spa Villas (indoor-outdoor treatment villas for one or two at Vista Spa) may be booked here, too.

Spa amenities include non-alcoholic beverages,

sandals and robes for use during treatments, lockers, steam room, sauna, locker room, showers, and more. A selection of beauty products is available for purchase. What follows is a sampling of treatments:

ELEMIS AROMA SPA OCEAN WRAP WITH HALF-BODY MASSAGE

The goal of this treatment is to help detox your body and restore balance and harmony. Stress is eased away with a combination of aromatherapy, a seaweed mask, and a blend of essential oils that is applied to your body before you are cocooned in a warm wrap. This is followed by a half-body massage. The ever-so-soothing treatment lasts about 75 minutes. Cost for the treatment is about $188.

HAIRDRESSING AND NAIL SERVICES

The salons offer hair styling, plus manicures and pedicures.

experience that is tailored to your body. Cost is about $118. The couples version of this treatment runs about $242.

TROPICAL RAIN FOREST
Experience the benefits of steam, heat, and water therapy combined with the power of aromatherapy to relax the mind and body. Pair it with a treatment and a visit costs just $9. A one-day pass is $16. Unlimited cruise passes are available, too (prices vary).

Chill Spa
(Dream and Fantasy)
A spa within a spa, Chill is a place reserved for teen guests. It offers a variety of spa services and treatments, including facials, massages, and manicures.

Reservations for Chill Spa may be made on-site any time after 1 P.M. on the first day of your cruise.

LA THERAPIE HYDRALIFT FACIAL
This "youth-enhancing" facial promises dramatic results. The appearance of fine lines and wrinkles is reduced, skin tone is restored, and the complexion is smoother. The 50-minute treatment costs $115.

SWEDISH MASSAGE
This 50-minute massage combines 10 cultural touches from around the world— including Swedish and deep tissue techniques—for an

PORTS OF CALL

To many travelers, the mere experience of being on board a ship is reward enough; to others, the destinations are the reason to sail. To us, it's a bit of each—so be it faraway places with strange-sounding names or luxurious beach resorts, these ports of call offer something for everyone.

We have made every effort to experience all of the "port adventures" that are detailed in this chapter, but new ones are always possible. For the scoop on the latest additions to the port and excursion lineup and, especially, for new home ports (i.e., Galveston and Miami) and Nova Scotia stops, visit *www.disneycruise.com*. That said, know that none of the port adventures are run by Disney Cruise Line—not even those on Castaway Cay. While Disney strives to oversee the manner in which they are operated, levels of excellence vary. On the pages that follow, you'll find an overview of each destination port and brief descriptions of select shore tours and adventures that are offered, followed by personal experiences. Remember, you have the freedom to wander about and experience all ports of call at your leisure. This chapter is just intended to provide guidance should you be interested in signing up for "organized" fun.

Be aware that the tours described here may change without notice; we hope the general descriptions and personal views will aid you in your selection. Enjoy.

CASTAWAY CAY

If you've ever dreamed of getting away to a private, tropical island, the folks at Disney have made it easy to fulfill the fantasy. Castaway Cay is a tiny island in the Abacos, one in the string of Bahamian isles. This little patch of paradise was secured for the sole use of passengers cruising on the Disney ships. It's small—only 3.1 miles long by 2.2 miles wide—and most of it was intentionally left undeveloped so that nature lovers can enjoy some still-unspoiled terrain.

Here you can take a ride in a glass-bottom boat or a fishing boat, go back to nature on a kayak adventure, try your wings at parasailing, or go snorkeling offshore—and then return to a barbecue feast. Of course, if you'd prefer to loll about in a palm-tree-shaded, beach-side hammock, refreshing beverage in hand, well, that can certainly be arranged.

Other island amenities include biking, beach games, organized activities for kids and teens; a shaded pavilion complete with billiards, ping-pong, basketball, shuffleboard, and more; Disney character greetings; plus a secluded, adults-only beach. The icing on the cake? How about renting an open-air massage in a private cabana overlooking the sea?

Returning guests (they always come back!) will be pleased to see that this happy place has gotten even happier —new additions include an expansion of the family beach, two water play areas known as Pelican Plunge and Spring-a-Leak, and nearly two dozen furnished beach cabanas.

Castaway Cay also has a post office, so you can tell the folks at home all about life on a private island.

Walking and Kayak Nature Adventure

(2.5–3 hours; Ages 10 and up)

Explore, learn, and take advantage of the island's natural wonders on this memorable adventure to the tranquil side of Castaway Cay. On the 40-minute walk to your kayak launch site you'll have your own personal guide to give you an inside look into the Bahamas' geology and history. Then you can work out your bi- and triceps on your one-hour kayak excursion through the ecologically sensitive mangrove environment. You'll even develop a sense of the importance of the mangrove ecosystem as a nursery for immature marine life and a habitat for birds.

As you stroke your oars through the shallow waters, you'll view a just-below-the-surface show starring tropical fish, sponges, and colorful coral formations. While you're there, enjoy a swim in the turquoise waters off a secluded sandy beach, where you may also explore the wonders of the seashore's tidal zones and their diverse vegetation. A 20-minute hike brings you back to your tram stop. A naturalist's nirvana, this tour is a must for the eco-minded among us.

What We Think *This was a nice tour for nature lovers—the younger sailors in our crew enjoyed it most of all. Some of us (the lazy ones!) would rather have relaxed out on the beach, but if Mother Nature's masterpieces are your cup of tea, this is the place to enjoy them all.*

⚓ Adults and children: $64 (ages 10 and above)

Glass-Bottom Boat Scenic Voyage
(1 hour; All ages)

This visit to the deep (without getting wet!) affords you a panoramic window to the world under the sea aboard a 46-foot, glass-bottom trawler. The hour-long narrated eco-tour gives passengers the skinny on what's happening down there. Best of all, the boat's expansive underwater windows provide a commanding view of the barrier reefs that protect Castaway Cay. It's fun to try and count the number of different types of fish, sea creatures, and coral you can spot during your journey.

What We Think *If you don't mind taking time away from the island, we thought this was an enjoyable experience. You do get a chance to see the island, look underwater and try to count the fish, and relax. If you are lucky enough to spot some dolphins and watch the guide feed them, it's more than worth your time; if not, well . . . that's in Mother Nature's hands, not ours. Our guide was great, very knowledgeable and friendly.* Note: *Seating on the boat is limited, so you should be able (and willing) to stand for long periods of time. Babies (and those tending them) won't enjoy this one.*

⚓ Adults: $35 (ages 10 and above)
   Children: $25 (ages 9 and under)

Sea Horse Catamaran Snorkel Adventure
(2–2.5 hours; Ages 5 and up)

Among the attractions of Castaway Cay are the colorful reefs that encircle it. Getting there really is half the fun, as a 63-foot catamaran whisks guests away to this snorkeling adventure. After receiving gear and a brief orientation, it's time to don those masks and dive in. Once you've dried off, enjoy complimentary snacks and beverages.

What We Think — *If you still haven't had your fill of snorkeling, give it a whirl—although some snorkeling snobs thought the fish weren't as spectacular as those at the other ports.*

⚓ Adults: $52 (ages 10 and above)
Children: $36 (ages 5–9)

Castaway Cay Bottom Fishing
(3–3.5 hours; Ages 6 and up)

This excursion gives guests the opportunity to enjoy the crystal clear waters of the Abaco Islands while anchored for a fishing experience. Tackle and bait are provided, along with water and soda. Be sure to bring a hat, camera, and sunscreen— and expect to be joined by up to seven other fisher-folk.

What We Think — *A new way to enjoy Castaway Cay, the fishing excursion gets a thumbs-up from enthusiastic anglers.*

⚓ Adults and children: $117 (ages 6 and above)

Snorkel Lagoon Equipment Rental
(All day; Ages 5 and up)

You're on your own on this one: Grab gear (at Gil's Fins and Boats or Flippers 'n' Floats) and put your face into the water of this 12-acre snorkel lagoon. Beginners can opt for Discover Trail, while more advanced water babies should follow the Explorer Trail. Snorkel awhile, rest on the beach, have some lunch, then snorkel some more—equipment rental is for the whole day. Snorkel, mask, fins, and vest are included. Kids under 13 must be accompanied by an adult at all times.

Ideal environment for snorkel novices and kids. There's even an underwater Mickey Mouse statue to search for!

⚓ Adults: $25 for 1 day; $31.25 for 2 days (ages 10 and above) Children: $10 for 1 day; $12.50 for 2 days (ages 5–9)

Watercraft Ski Adventure
(1 hour; Ages 8 and up)

What's it like to live on Castaway Cay? Here's your chance to find out. Board a personal watercraft and listen as a guide shares stories about the island's marine life, ecology, and storied history. Then it's off to a second destination, where your guide will describe the colorful history and environment of the Bahamas. Water shoes or sandals are the preferred footwear. Eyeglass straps come in handy, too. Note that riders board from the water—dress appropriately.

Brief, but memorable. Lots of colorful photo ops. The boats are fun!

⚓ $95 for single riders; $160 for double riders. Guests must be age 8 or older to ride, 18 and up to drive, 16 with a parent's permission.

135

Float/Tube Rentals
(All day; Ages 5 and up)

If doing absolutely nothing sounds good to you, rent a tube or float and bob in the gently rolling waves of a lagoon. The water is crystal clear and, best of all, rentals are good for the whole day! Children under 13 years of age must be accompanied by an adult. Floats and tubes can be picked up at the Flippers 'n' Floats. (Grown-ups can also get them at Windsock Hut at Serenity Bay.) Don't forget the sunscreen.

What We Think

What's not to love? Take it all in—soon you're back in the real world.

⚓ Adults and children: $6 for 1 day;
   $7.50 for 2 days (ages 5 and above)

Parasailing
(45 minutes, airborne 5–7 minutes; Ages 8 and up)

On this once-in-a-lifetime experience, you get a high-flying view of the world around you as you soar approximately 600 to 1,000 feet above Castaway Cay. You'll enjoy a whole new perspective of the landscape—and the boats that look more like bathtub toys. Although the entire flight lasts only five to seven minutes, the preparation for the adventure and landing encompasses about 45 minutes. It's an experience you won't soon forget. A couple of restrictions: Guests must weigh more than 90 pounds, but must not exceed 375 pounds. Children under 13 must be accompanied by an adult. Non-flying guardians stay on the boat while each participant takes a trip into the sky. Note that this excursion will be canceled if weather conditions are not ideal.

What We Think — *One member of our hardy crew—at the tender age of 65—recently took to the skies on this aerial adventure. Not only did she live to tell about it, she said it was one of the most exhilarating experiences she'd ever had. And she told us . . . and she told us . . . and she's still telling us. Others found the experience a little scary, but thrilling. It really feels as though you're flying, but it's so gentle that you aren't always aware that you're moving. "Memorable" was the word from all who had their heads in the clouds.*

⚓ Adults and children:
    $79 (ages 8 and above)

HOT TIP

Keep your cameras and valuables dry with specially designed water-proof bags available from L.L. Bean, Magellan's, and other retailers.

Hide Out
(All day; Ages 14–17)

This secluded area is zoned for teens only. The popular teen retreat, mere steps from the crystal clear waters of the Caribbean, has colorful deck chairs—perfect for soaking up sun, listening to music, or watching the nearby volleyball and soccer action. Food, soft drinks, and snacks (including ice cream) are available.

What We Think *How cool is it that teens have their own space on Castaway Cay? Here they can chill without being pestered by younger siblings.*

⚓ Teens only: free

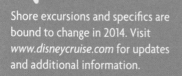

HOT TIP

Shore excursions and specifics are bound to change in 2014. Visit *www.disneycruise.com* for updates and additional information.

Bicycle Rentals
(1 hour; All ages)

Don your helmet and enjoy a two-wheeled tour of Disney's private island. Bikes are available for rent by the hour, and there are child seats available for the little ones. Children must be able to ride a two-wheel bike and are required to wear (provided) helmets.

What We Think *This was an excellent family experience for all. Little ones sat at the rear of grown-ups' bikes, while older children had their own bikes. The roads aren't the smoothest, but everyone said that it was a fun hour's diversion.*

⚓ Adults and children:
   $6 per hour

Castaway Cay Getaway Package
(All day; Ages 5 and up)

For active folks who want to snorkel and bike about this Disney isle, here's an all-inclusive package that lets you frolic to your heart's content. You'll receive snorkeling equipment and float rental for the day, plus a one-hour bicycle rental. Kids under age 13 must be accompanied by an adult.

Since it's pretty much a given that you'll want to snorkel, float, and splash in the ocean, or pedal about the island, the only real question to ask yourself is: Will I want to do all three? If the answer is an enthusiastic yes, then we say go for it!

⚓ Adults: $32 for 1 day; $40 for 2 days (ages 10 and above)
Children: $16 for 1 day; $20 for 2 days (ages 5–9)

Extreme Getaway Package
(All day; Ages 5 and up)

As with the Castaway Cay Getaway Package, this is not for lazy beach bums. The all-inclusive deal lets you have it all (well, most of it!). You'll get snorkeling equipment and float rental for the day, a one-hour stingray encounter, plus a one-hour bicycle rental. And, yes, there will be some time for you to snooze in the sun, too! Children under the age of 13 must be accompanied by an adult.

Too much of a good thing? Nah. You simply can't get enough of Castaway Cay. We find this package "extreme"-ly enjoyable.

⚓ Adults: $54 (ages 10 and above)
Children: $39 (ages 5–9)

The Wild Side
(4 hours; Ages 14–17)

Attention, teens! Here is an adventure designed exclusively for you. Venture into uncharted territory as you explore the wild side of the island, where you can snorkel, bike ride, and sea-kayak on your own. No moms, dads, or baby brothers and sisters here.

 What We Think *The teens who came back from this trip had nothing but good things to say about it; it was a special time to spend with old friends and new, and enjoy some grown-up hours away from parents and siblings. Awesome!*

⚓ Teens: $35 (14–17 only)

Boat Rentals
(30 minutes; Ages 5 and up)

For those who can't get enough of the Bahamian waters, a variety of boats are available for rent at Gil's Fins and Boats. All craft are subject to availability. They can't be reserved in advance—it's all walk-up rental only. Children under age 13 must be accompanied by an adult. All prices are for a half-hour rental, per person:

Paddleboats: 2-seater, $8; 4-seater, $10. Sea Kayak: 1-seater, $8; 2-seater, $10. Aqua Fin: $15. Aqua Trike: $15. Hobie Cat: $18.

What We Think *Your choice. It's all here. Paddle (or pedal) to your heart's content.*

⚓ Adults and children: $8–$20 per half hour (ages 5 and above)

In Da Shade Game Pavilion
(All day; All ages)

Need a break from the sun? We've got just the place for you—Castaway Cay's Grouper Game Room. Located near Castaway Cay family beach, it is a *shaded* game room and recreation area where guests of all ages can play table tennis, basketball, shuffleboard, foosball, giant checkers, a game of pool, and more. Happy news for Mom and Dad: These are fun and *free* activities.

What We Think *A surefire hit with kids, we've noticed more than a few grown-ups enjoying themselves in these parts, too. Table tennis, anyone?*

⚓ Adults and children: free

Castaway Ray's Stingray Adventure
(1 hour; Ages 5 and up)

Get up close and personal with Southern stingrays in Castaway Cay's private lagoon. (Don't worry, they can't sting.) The guided encounter (a human "Ray" is your guide) includes a background session about these interesting sea creatures and snorkel instruction. The adventure culminates with a chance to feed, touch, and swim with the rays.

What We Think *We know every minute on Castaway Cay is precious, but this is an hour well spent. We'll play with the rays any day.*

⚓ Adults: $35 (ages 10 and above)
   Children: $29 (ages 5–9)

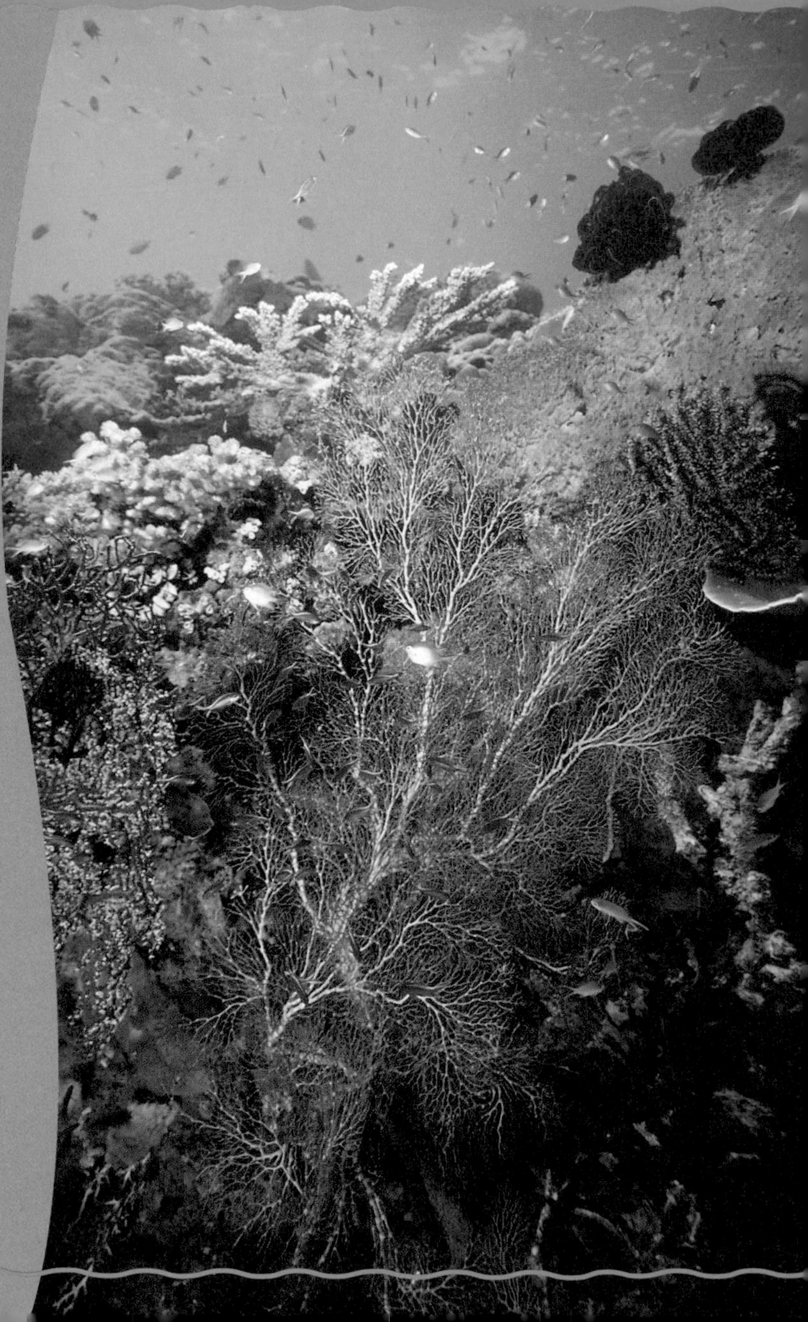

COZUMEL

Welcome to the biggest island in Mexico! The 28-mile-long island, which gets its name from the Mayan phrase *cuzam huzil*, meaning "land of the swallows," is in the Caribbean, just 12 miles off the mainland. Home to the Palancar Reef (the second-largest diving reef in the world), it's no wonder that Cozumel is a magnet for underwater explorers and snorkelers.

Legend and lore abound here. Centuries ago, in about 300 A.D., the island was a shrine to Ixchel, the goddess of the moon and fertility. (It is said that when angered, she vents her wrath through violent hurricanes and torrential rains. So don't make her angry. . . .)

The area is still rich in ancient sites. Here you will discover the history of a centuries-old culture in its ruins and churches—echoes of the past just waiting for modern-day explorers.

Cozumel is a scuba diver's paradise (it was a favorite destination of the late undersea explorer Jacques Cousteau). Its splendid coral reefs and tropical fish make it irresistible to divers, and fishing aficionados won't be disappointed, either: The island's 600-feet-deep waters are populated by marlin, grouper, mackerel, and sailfish—in fact, several world sailfish records have been set here. Actually, it's a place for everyone—even golfers can satisfy an urge here. Intrigued? Read on.

143

Dolphin Kids at Dolphinaris
(3 hours; Ages 4–9)

After a kid-friendly intro to dolphins (including a discussion of anatomy, physiology, and history), guests experience a close encounter with Pacific bottlenose dolphins. Under the supervision of a trainer, children enjoy 40 minutes of interacting with the friendly mammals. The experience is capped with a little dolphin showboating (kisses, hugs, and jumps). Kids must be accompanied by a parent or guardian.

What We Think *Thrilling for most youngsters, though some little ones might be a bit spooked by the up-close encounter with the enormous creatures. They may also get squirmy during the lesson. Older kids dig it.*

⚓ Children: $105 (ages 4–9)

Dolphin Push, Pull, and Swim
(3–5.5 hours; Ages 5 and up)

Cozumel offers plenty of dolphin fun, but this adventure adds another dimension—a swift ride on a boogie board while tethered to the pectoral flippers of a dolphin. The fun happens at Chankanaab National Park, where you also can put on a mask and swim with the friendly dolphins. You'll quickly find that it's easy to fall in love with these smart and graceful marine animals.

What We Think *Just climb on and ride— this is an easy, safer step beyond the belly ride offered with other Cozumel dolphin experiences.*

⚓ Adults: $132 (ages 10 and above)
    Children: $109 (ages 5–9)

Atlantis Submarine Expedition
(2.5 hours; Ages 4 and up)

Get a fish's-eye view of the colorful world under the sea, thanks to the U.S. Coast Guard–certified submarine *Atlantis*. As the sub dives 110 feet into the deep, guests see tropical fish and towering coral formations, while a narrator makes the wonder of it all even more wonderful. Once the boat surfaces, passengers will have yet another treat—free rum and fruit punch.

What We Think *We met some parents who took their kids (ages 6 and 10) down under. They found it to be a kid-friendly experience. And although we enjoyed the tour, we recommend that claustrophobes avoid this one.*

⚓ Adults: $99 (ages 10 and above) Children: $57 (ages 4–9; must be at least 36 inches tall)

Fury Catamaran Sail, Snorkel, and Beach Party
(4.5–5 hours; Ages 5 and up)

Enjoy the best of all possible worlds on this outing. Your magic carpet is a luxurious 65-foot catamaran replete with sundeck and shady areas. The day includes a snorkeling adventure (all equipment provided) and a beach party complete with kayaks and volleyball. If that's not enough, complimentary soft drinks are yours for the asking, as are margaritas and beer (as long as you're at least 21 years of age).

What We Think *Adventurous types, especially teens, love this one. After the snorkeling, the party really gets under way—and the grown-ups find the margaritas marvelous.*

⚓ Adults: $58 (ages 10 and above) Children: $31 (ages 5–9)

Tulum Ruins
(7–7.5 hours; Ages 5 and up)

Imagine leaving your cruise ship and (after a 45-minute ferry ride) boarding a bus to the past. That's what you'll do on this archaeological tour. The sacred Mayan city of Tulum is the destination, a knowledgeable guide is your invaluable companion, and the remnants of a fascinating civilization are yours to explore. There's a bit of time to enjoy the nearby beach, and soft drinks and sandwiches are included in the price of the tour. A few notes: There is an additional charge to use *your own* video camera. Since the terrain is not stroller-friendly (read: *not allowed*) and requires a lot of walking, this tour is not recommended for children under age 8.

What We Think *While fascinating, this is a very long day. Our guide was informative, but our hardy crew agreed that this is best left to the archaeological-minded traveler. Kids may get restless—there's a lot of travel time.*

⚓ Adults: $99 (ages 10 and above)
   Children: $75 (ages 5–9)

Cozumel Ruins and Beach Tour
(4–4.5 hours; Ages 5 and up)

Culture and leisure go hand in hand on this guided tour where you explore the ancient history of Cozumel at the San Gervasio Ruins, a Mayan religious center, and then chill out at Playa Mia Adventure Park for an hour and a half of swimming and water sports (there is an additional charge for equipment). The terrain is rough here, so strollers are not allowed. Beverages arc included, and food may be purchased.

What We Think — *The terrain wasn't only too rough for baby strollers—it was tough for adult "strollers," too.*

⚓ Adults: $52 (ages 10 and above)
  Children: $35 (ages 5–9)

Dolphin Swim at Dolphinaris
(3 hours; Ages 5 and up)

Following a brief dolphin lesson, guests make their way to a submerged (waist-deep) platform and enjoy an in-water exchange with real live bottlenose dolphins. You'll learn how dolphins respond to hand signals, get some hands-on time with the crafty mammals, and even share a kiss with one of your newfound friends (or a handshake for the modest). The bonding continues in the deeper coves area, where everyone is treated to a belly-ride, courtesy of our fine flippered friends.

What We Think — *For us, 40 minutes of quality time with these magical creatures is priceless—though the actual price is a bit hefty! Still, it's a gem of an experience.*

⚓ Adults: $146 (ages 10 and above)
  Children: $117 (ages 5–9)

GRAND CAYMAN

In 1503, when Christopher Columbus came upon these islands (there are actually three Caymans: Grand Cayman, at 76 square miles, is the largest; Little Cayman; and Cayman Brac), he named them *Las Tortugas*, a nod to the then-large turtle population here. The present name is closer to *caymanas*, the Spanish-Carib word for alligators, although the nearest relatives you'll find here are iguanas. What you *will* find are big bucks (the paper kind, that is). George Town, the capital city, is one of the world's largest financial centers, home to more than 500 banks.

Of much greater interest to leisure travelers is that the sparkling waters off its Caribbean shores make Grand Cayman a snorkeler's and diver's dream. In fact, it's one of the top five dive destinations in the world.

Waters teem with coral and fish, and even non-swimmers can get a view of these underwater wonders—including the Cayman Wall and its resident population of stingrays—from a glass-bottom boat or mini-sub.

Shoppers should head for Fort Street and Cardinal Avenue. *Note:* Although you may be tempted, steer clear of all items made from turtle and black coral. Both are endangered species. In fact, items made from sea turtle cannot be brought back to the United States. Opt instead for some of the interesting jewelry fashioned from shipwreck artifacts—some old gold pieces, perhaps? And if hunger strikes, have lunch in town. Our favorite island treat is conch (pronounced *konk*)—as fritters or in chowder. Trust us, it's delicious.

Island Tour and Snorkeling with Stingrays
(4.5 hours; Ages 5 and up)

A veritable smorgasbord of adventures, this tour lets you do it all in a scant 4 hours. First, it's a stop at world-famous Seven Mile Beach, then a chance to experience classic island architecture, and, for nature lovers, a visit to the Cayman Turtle Farm. Naturalists will appreciate the island's prehistoric rock formation, a place the locals call "Hell." And last, but certainly not least, head to Stingray Sandbar to get up close and personal with sea life. Snorkeling equipment is provided.

What We Think *The turtle farm was just okay, but the snorkeling made up for it. You gotta love those stingrays.*

⚓ Adults: $72 (ages 10 and above)
   Children: $56 (ages 5–9)

Pirate Encounter
(2.5 hours; Ages 3 and up)

This excursion could be called "We Wanna Walk the Plank!" A short tender-boat trip takes guests to one of the world's last wooden brigs, *Valhalla*. Friendly pirates are there to welcome you aboard, sail the ship past Seven Mile Beach, and make you walk *to* the plank (don't worry, you don't have to jump, but you should—it's a lot of fun!). Figure on about 40 minutes of splashing-around time.

What We Think *Who knew how much fun it would be to jump off the side of a pirate ship —again and again and again?! It's not for guests with limited mobility, but young'uns love the pirate factor.*

⚓ Adults: $42 (ages 10 and above)
   Children: $28 (ages 3–9)

Seven Mile Beach Break
(4 hours; All ages)

A short air-conditioned bus ride is all it takes to get to Grand Cayman's newest beach destination: Sea Grape Beach. So grab a lounge chair (no extra charge), a complimentary soft drink, sit back, relax, and enjoy. Take some cash, as there's an opportunity to buy grilled snacks and various beverages. Water-sport equipment rentals are also available.

What We Think *A beach day we can get excited about! The transportation-beach time ratio is just right, as is the area of beach that's reserved for Disney Cruise Line guests. And the price is right, too.*

⚓ Adults: $36 (ages 10 and above)
   Children: $26 (ages 3–9)
   Under age 3: free

Shipwreck and Reef Snorkeling
(2.5 hours; Ages 5 and up)

First stop is the *Callie*, one of the Caymans' most famous wrecks. On board, experienced dive masters provide a history of the ship, plus give those who need it some instruction in snorkeling. The next stop affords guests the opportunity to view some spectacular coral reef formations and tropical fish; you might even spot a turtle. Snorkeling equipment, ice water, and lemonade are provided.

What We Think *This tour proved a major favorite among our scouts. They loved the snorkeling and the shipwreck—and one of them saw a huge turtle. Totally excellent.*

⚓ Adults: $39 (ages 10 and above)
   Children: $31 (ages 5–9)

Nautilus Undersea Tour and Reef Snorkel
(3 hours; Ages 5 and up)

Here's an opportunity to see the sea from both above and below. On board the *Nautilus*, the world's largest semi-submarine, you'll sail over some spectacular shipwrecks and out to Cheeseburger Reef. As for the "below" part of the adventure: Don your goggles and snorkel with the rainbow of tropical fish that call this home. Snorkel gear is included.

What We Think *"A nice day" was mostly what we heard about this tour. Folks expected more when they heard the word "Nautilus" (like deep dives and so on), but they generally enjoyed the time and felt it was worth the money.*

⚓ Adults: $52 (ages 10 and above)
  Children: $43 (ages 5–9)

Stingray City Reef Sail and Snorkel
(3.5 hours; Ages 5 and up)

No mere dip-your-face-in-the-water-near-the-shore experience, this seven-mile adventure aboard a 65-foot catamaran gives you an opportunity to explore the deep, study the coral formations, and watch fish cavort before your eyes. All snorkeling equipment, water, and soft drinks are provided.

What We Think *Members of our group went on this tour and gave it high marks. The snorkeling location for this one was peaceful, and a knowledgeable guide enriched the experience immensely. A good time was had by all— even the fish.*

⚓ Adults: $60 (ages 10 and above)
  Children: $47 (ages 5–9)

Boatswain's Adventure Marine Park
(4.5–5 hours; All ages)

Turtles, lizards, and sharks—oh, my! You'll see them all at Boatswain's Adventure Marine Park. The shoreside retreat is home to more than 11,000 turtles at the historic Cayman Turtle Farm. There's also a 1.3 million-gallon lagoon that's teeming with wildlife. You may take a stroll down the Nature Trail (if you want to see those lizards), shop on Cayman Street, and/or dive into Breaker's lagoon. Snorkel equipment is provided, food is not (though it is possible to buy some).

It's a bit pricey, but you get a lot for the money. A must for turtle fans.

⚓ Adults: $92 (ages 10 and above)
Children: $72 (ages 3–9)
Under age 3: free

Grand Cayman Island Tour
(2 hours; All ages)

Although most folks head for the island's shores, the curious explorer should know that Grand Cayman is more than a beach—much more. And you'll discover this on an air-conditioned bus that meanders through the quaint streets of George Town and past the storybook-perfect gingerbread houses to the odd rock formations of the eerie island wonder called "Hell." Then it's on to the world's only turtle breeding operation of its kind, Cayman Turtle Farm.

We were a little disappointed in this one. The turtles were interesting, but not worth the outing.

⚓ Adults: $39 (ages 10 and above)
Children: $29 (ages 3–9)
Under age 3: free

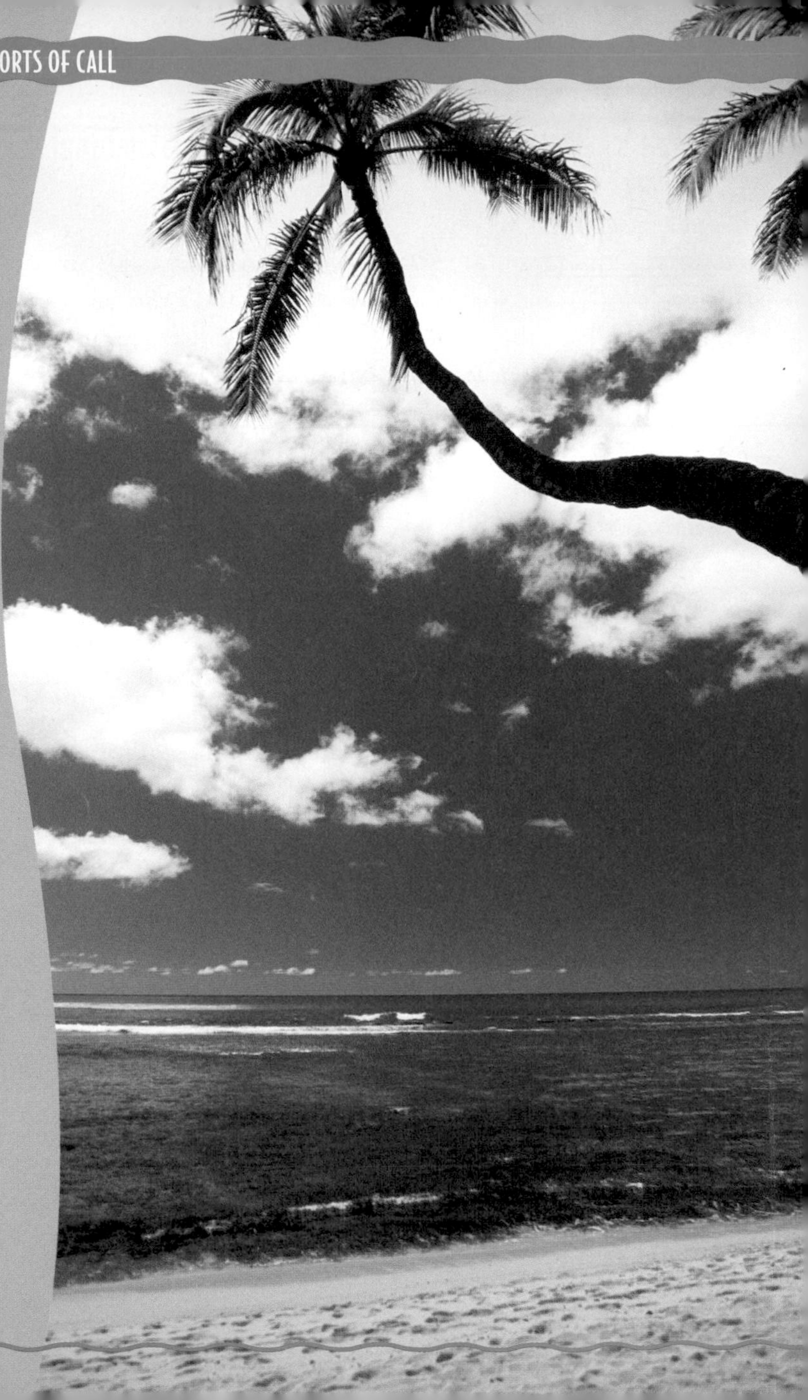

KEY WEST

The southernmost community in the continental U.S. and yet closer to Havana, Cuba, than it is to Miami, Key West is a charming blend of the best of southern, Bahamian, Cuban, and Yankee food, architecture, and hospitality.

Discovered (along with the rest of Florida) by Ponce de León, and a favorite destination of fishermen, artists, and writers, this tiny piece of land was home for 30 years to Ernest Hemingway (who, among other works, penned *To Have and Have Not* and *For Whom the Bell Tolls* here). President Harry Truman had his "little White House" here, and Tennessee Williams, John Dos Passos, and Robert Frost found these friendly climes ideal for their creative and leisure liking. In fact, travelers can still visit Hemingway's Spanish Colonial–style house and lush gardens, and the Harry S. Truman Little White House Museum.

By all means, take the tour train or the trolley to orient yourself, but once you've done that, Key West is best explored on foot—stop and admire the architecture—from Bahamian wooden gingerbread houses to those of New England sea captains, complete with widow's watch. The oldest house in Key West, circa 1829, was owned by a sea captain; you can still tour it and see its ship models, furnished dollhouse, and seafaring documents. For shoppers, galleries and crafts shops abound, as do lots and lots of places to buy T-shirts. Or do what most everyone else does and take to the water—be it by glass-bottom boat, catamaran, or kayak.

Key West Catamaran Sail & Snorkel Tour
(3.5 hours; Ages 5 and up)

If you're the seafaring sort, this is the best way to experience the magic of Key West. You'll enjoy a 3-hour sailing adventure that includes snorkeling amid vibrant coral and tropical fish. Equipment and instruction are provided, as are beverages. Snorkeling is off the back of the catamaran in water that's about 15 to 20 feet deep.

What We Think
Good marks were given by all the guests who took this tour.

⚓ Adults: $49 (ages 10 and above)
Children: $28 (ages 5–9)

The Key West Butterfly & Nature Conservatory with Aquarium
(Duration varies; All ages)

For those who crave serenity (now!), this excursion has your name on it. After a short walk and shuttle ride, guests enjoy a stroll through a tropical paradise. The climate-controlled environment is home to more than 50 species of butterfly, plus exotic and flowering plants and cascading waterfalls. After the tour, guests are transported to the Key West Aquarium—the original tourist attraction in the Florida Keys.

What We Think
We love this excursion. The Butterfly Conservatory is very interesting and serene. We overheard lots of "oohing" and "aahing" from kids and grown-ups alike. The aquarium delivers, too. They let you pet the sharks!

⚓ Adults: $43 (ages 10 and above)
Children: $28 (ages 3–9)
Under age 3: free

Glass-Bottom Boat Tour on the Pride of Key West
(2.5 hours; All ages)

Perfectly named, the *Pride of Key West* is a 65-foot, glass-bottom catamaran that gives passengers an incomparable view of the underwater world of the Keys. And comfort is key here, too: There are upper and lower sundecks, a large climate-controlled viewing area, and restrooms. A big plus is the narrated ecotour of North America's only living coral reef. Sit back, relax, and enjoy. Snacks and beverages are available to buy.

 Comfort with a capital C is the key word to this Key tour. And the narration was a major plus.

⚓ Adults: $42 (ages 10 and above)
   Children: $25 (ages 9 and under)

Presidents, Pirates, & Pioneers
(2 hours; Ages 3 and up)

Step back in time during this walking tour and discover the stories behind some of the city's most famous places, including the Shipwreck Historeum Museum and the Harry S. Truman Little White House. The tour concludes with complimentary conch fritters and bottled water. In all, expect to walk about 1.5 miles. Wheelchairs are permitted, but the Shipwreck Historeum is not wheelchair accessible.

This is a nice way to soak up a bit of history and get some exercise to boot. Wear comfortable walking shoes! A good tour guide makes all the difference in the world.

⚓ Adults: $38 (ages 10 and above)
   Children: $23 (ages 3–9)

PRACTICAL PACKAGE DEALS

Too lazy to take pictures? Think about springing for the Photography Package. For one lump sum, pictures of your family with Mickey, Minnie, Chip and Dale, and even Cinderella can grace your family photo album without you clicking a finger.

Wine lovers should be aware of Disney's wine packages; when you pre-pay for several bottles at a time, you save big bucks.

Beer drinkers may purchase a "refillable mug," good for discount suds throughout the cruise.

President Truman's Key West
(2–2.5 hours; All ages)

Key West was President Truman's home away from home. To that end, he even had a "Little White House"— the beautifully restored starting point for this tour.

It's about a five-minute walk to the trolley (or train). Once aboard, you'll pass sites such as Ernest Hemingway's home and museum (and maybe spot an ancestor of his six-toed cats), the Audubon House museum, and the schooner *Western Union*. In all, more than 100 points of interest are touched upon. It involves a bit of walking along the way, so wear comfy shoes.

 This is an ambitious but informative tour. The often enlightening experience is better for more mature travelers, as kids tend to get a bit antsy.

Adults: $46 (ages 10 and above)
Children: $25 (ages 3–9)
Under age 3: Free

Snorkel, Kayak, & Dolphin-Watching Adventure
(3.5–4 hours; Ages 5 and up)

A 20-minute boat ride deposits guests at Key West Wildlife Refuge—home to a vast array of marine life and small outlying islands. The adventure begins by paddling through winding mangroves. Next up? A shallow-water snorkel by a shipwreck (a remnant of 2005's Hurricane Wilma). Afterward, you'll head to an area known as the "Dolphin Playground." It's home to about 100 bottlenose dolphins. Have those cameras ready!

The refuge is lovely, the snorkeling is swell, and spotting dolphins is the best! Of course, there's always a chance they'll be camera shy.

⚓ Adults: $95 (ages 10 and above)
Children: $85 (ages 5–9)

WILL YOU MARRY ME—AGAIN?

Whether you're celebrating your first, fifteenth, or fiftieth, renewing your vows can be a life-affirming experience. Those couples who still feel like newlyweds long after the wedding day know that anniversaries can mark more than years. What better way to say "I love you still" than by having another wedding? Perhaps your first "I do's" were said in front of a justice of the peace; now you can don that white gown and do it up in grand style. Or, if you prefer to keep it low-key, a small corsage and boutonniere will do just fine. A ship's officer can perform the ceremony. Ask the kids along this time (chances are they weren't present for the first go-round), or make it a very private affair with just the two of you, as it was at the beginning. We can't tell you how many couples have decided to renew their vows on the Disney ships; suffice it to say that there's a lot of hand-holding, slow dancing, and stolen kisses to be seen on deck. For additional information, call 321-939-4610.

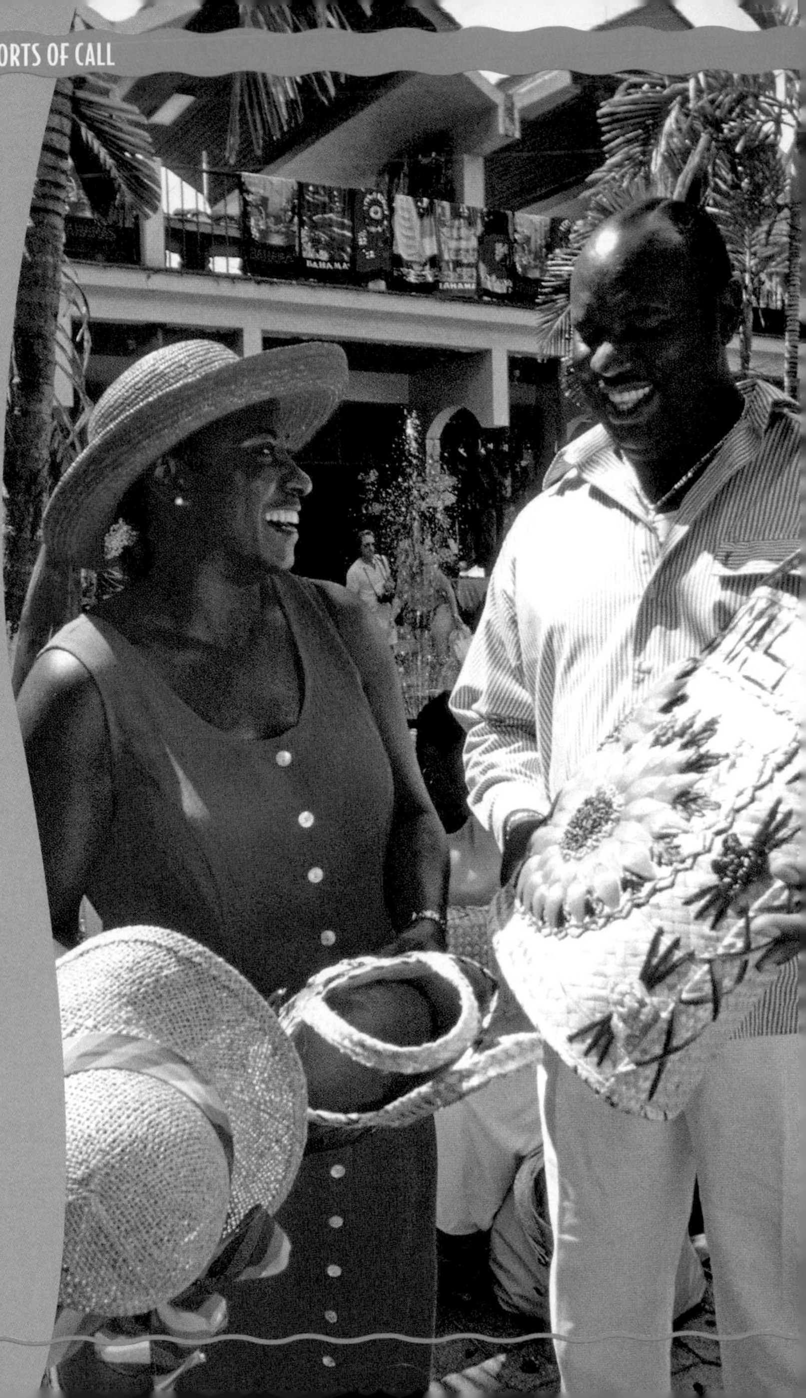

NASSAU

Is it really better in the Bahamas? That depends on who you ask! Within this island paradise, you will find places to shop, swim, snorkel, sail, gamble, and sip a cool, refreshing beverage while looking out over a turquoise ocean. (Some say the shopping district is sensational, others find it uninspired—different strokes for different folks.)

Beaches are plentiful, but for those who like to venture beyond the sand, there are places here—where goats outnumber TV sets, where the roads are not-so-smooth, and the ferries are off schedule more than on—that take you to the "true" Bahamas, where Bahamians do their traditional dance (the *junkanoo*), and *goombay* music fills the air. This is where you can sample authentic island cooking (lots of grouper, lobster, conch, and johnnycakes) and take a turn at going local, if only for a few hours.

There are actually about 200 islands and some 2,000 tiny islands known as cays (pronounced *keys*) in the Bahamas, all scattered across 100,000 square miles of the Atlantic Ocean. The adventures that are described on the following pages are available to you in Nassau, the island nation's capital. Aside from its divine diving, rich in shipwrecks, there is much more to see in the Bahamas—be it lush gardens and waterfalls, or Victorian mansions and 17th-century Georgian buildings. The good news is that, for the most part, the island's pride in its heritage is reflected in the way it is maintained.

Atlantis Aquaventure
(5–8 hours; All ages)

The excursion begins with a 25-minute bus ride and an escorted walk (about 20 minutes) to the 63-acre water park at the Atlantis resort. Following a guided tour of an underwater aquarium, you're free to enjoy the waterslides, river rapids, pools, and more. Water bikes, kayaks, and snorkel equipment may be rented. A light lunch is included. You'll have access to a beach, shopping, and a casino, too. Guests must be at least 48 inches tall to ride the waterslides. Swim diapers are a must for babies.

 Water park fans will not be disappointed (well, unless the weather is crummy). It's a bit of a splurge, but we're not complaining. (Yeah, we love water parks.)

⚓ Adults: $169 (ages 10 and above)
Children: $115 (ages 3–9)
Under age 3: free

Blue Lagoon Sea Lion Encounter
(4–4.5 hours; Ages 8 and up)

Blue Lagoon Island—a 30-minute catamaran ride away—is one of the world's few marine mammal centers that offers the opportunity to interact with sea lions. The experience includes a lesson about these gentle, intelligent animals and a 30-minute visit in a specially designed, waist-deep pool. After you hug your new friend good-bye, say hi to the bottlenose dolphins that live nearby. (Human) food is available for purchase. Guests must be at least 38 inches tall to participate.

Sea lions can be quite affectionate. Who knew? This experience is a home run for animal lovers.

⚓ Adults: $115 (ages 10 and above)
Children: $109 (ages 8–9; children ages 8–12 must be accompanied by a parent or guardian)

Catamaran Sail and Reef Snorkeling
(3.5–4 hours; Ages 5 and up)

The lush, tropical reef you'll find at your destination is the icing on the cake for this half-day outing: The catamaran, complete with its shaded lounge and spacious deck area, takes you on a cruise through historic Nassau Harbor. If you can tear yourself away from the view, you'll receive snorkel instructions (equipment is included) from the knowledgeable crew who, for your safety, also accompany you into the water.

 We give this one a big thumbs-up. The boat was small, the instructions were thorough, and the fish were plentiful —what more could one ask? Okay, the water was a bit chilly, but still . . .

⚓ Adults: $49 (ages 10 and above)
Children: $34 (ages 5–9)

Blue Lagoon Island Beach Day
(4.5–7.5 hours; All ages)

A double-decker catamaran takes you to a private island where you'll take a short stroll to a protected lagoon with a sugary beach for swimming, kayaking, or water biking—or just claim a hammock and relax. See dolphins and sea lions in a natural ocean habitat at Dolphin Encounters. Lunch is included (but cocktails are extra).

 A blissful way to spend the day—and the perfect beach for little ones.

⚓ Adults: $69 (ages 10 and above)
Children: $55 (ages 9 and under; children must be accompanied by a parent or guardian)

ST. MAARTEN

Some call it St. Maarten, while others insist upon St. Martin. And they're both right. During the 1600s, after centuries of battles over dominance, Spain bowed out and the deadlocked Dutch and French agreed to disagree and split this small island in half—well, not quite half: The French got 21 square miles and the Dutch, 16. (Legends abound as to why, but our favorite is that the two countries decided to claim their territory by conducting a race around the island, and the French won.)

St. Maarten—the Dutch side of the island, and one of the world's only land masses owned by two countries—is the lively sector, while St. Martin—the bucolic French side, larger but more serene—attracts visitors who crave peace and tranquility, with some gourmet food thrown in for good measure. Both sides boast abundant beaches and sparkling waters. Shoppers enjoy Philipsburg's no-tax-on-imported-goods policy. Lots of shops are downright tacky, but with a little effort you can manage to part with some green stuff during your stay. And, of course, there's gambling. Casinos line the area by the pier, and most of the Dutch-side hotels offer games of chance. The French, meanwhile, have bouillabaisse and onion soup. So it's possible to swim anywhere, have a meal on either side of the island, and either go to a club in Marigot (the French capital) or play the slots on the Dutch side. Whatever you choose, the cards are stacked in your favor on this *très* continental isle.

Island Drive and Explorer Cruise
(4 hours; All ages)

Here you can enjoy the best of all worlds—visit Simpsons Bay Lagoon, and then board the *Explorer* for a half-hour cruise to Marigot, the island's French capital. Sightsee and shop, and then take the scenic return to Philipsburg, the Dutch capital, where you can do some more sightseeing and shopping. Too history heavy? Not a bit. Expensive? Only if you can't resist the shopping scene. Let your budget—and your willpower—be your guide.

This was interesting—if you're into learning about island history. If you'd rather hit the beach, look elsewhere. We loved the French side, although Philipsburg is not without its charms.

⚓ Adults: $49 (ages 10 and above)
    Children: $24 (ages 9 and under)

St. Maarten Island & Butterfly Farm Tour
(3.5 hours; All ages)

Originating in Philipsburg, this narrated bus tour offers stunning scenery and, best of all, a visit to a butterfly farm on the island's French side. Once you have had your fill of the fluttery creatures, you can fritter away time in Marigot, where markets, cafés, and duty-free shops are all at your disposal.

An enjoyable experience, but many agree that it's a bit too long—definitely not worth the hours away from potential beach time.

⚓ Adults: $38 (ages 10 and above)
    Children: $28 (ages 3–9)
    Under age 3: free

Mountain Top Downhill Rainforest Trek
(3.5–4 hours; Ages 8 and up)

Good walking shoes are a must for this half-day outing in the wild. Your guide will familiarize you with the wonders of the wilderness as you ride in an open-air safari vehicle on your way to the heights—by island standards—of Pic Paradise. Your reward? Breathtaking 360-degree views of St. Maarten and its seven neighboring islands. After that, it's time for an all-downhill trek into the depths of St. Maarten's only rainforest. The hike—which takes approximately two hours—covers ancient trails under the canopy of 200-year-old trees. Guests are treated to sights such as a long-abandoned sugar plantation and, quite possibly, monkeys, a mongoose or two, and more than a few iguanas. Guests should be in good physical condition to participate in this trek—it's not terribly strenuous, but it does involve quite a bit of walking over irregular, sometimes steep, terrain.

While the scenery is gorgeous, it was just too darn hot for us to get much out of the experience. We'll try it again during a cooler time of year. It's fun to search for monkeys!

⚓ Adults: $65 (ages 10 and above)
  Children: $58 (ages 8–9)

Afternoon Beach Bash Tour
(3.5–4 hours; All ages)

It takes about 30 minutes to reach Orient Bay by bus, but the payoff for your patience is about two full hours of fun in the sun on one of the Caribbean's best beaches. Fruit punch and rum punch are free flowing (literally—there's no charge), while water-sport equipment, parasailing, hair-braiding, and massages are available for an extra charge. Food and additional beverages may be purchased at any of the full-service restaurants or beach bars. Note that nudity or topless bathing may be encountered.

What We Think *All in all, an enjoyable beach day—and an excellent value. Not for the modest (see above note!).*

⚓ Adults: $41 (ages 10 and above)
Children: $22 (ages 3–9)
Under age 3: free

Golden Eagle Catamaran
(4 hours; Ages 5 and up)

The beautiful Caribbean is yours for the swimming— or snorkeling (equipment provided) or sunbathing— on a relaxing ride that concludes with pastries and an open bar.

What We Think *A pleasant way to pass the time in the Caribbean. It was very laid-back, and if that's what you yearn for, this is for you.*

⚓ Adults: $82 (ages 10 and above)
Children: $46 (ages 5–9)

Seaworld Explorer–Coral Reef Exploration
(2.5 hours; Ages 3 and up)

Here's your chance to spy on sea creatures without getting the least bit water-logged. A 45-minute voyage on the semi-submarine *Seaworld Explorer* lets guests ooh and aah at aquatic life in its natural habitat and when some of it's brought aboard the vessel, courtesy of a skilled diver/sea critter wrangler. Beverages are included, but you may want to pack a snack. Unfortunately, wheelchairs cannot be accommodated aboard the vessel.

What We Think *The commute-time to fun-time ratio is a bit lopsided for our taste. But if you fancy yourself a semi-sub fan, it just may make your day. Claustrophobes, however, should sit this one out.*

⚓ Adults: $45 (ages 10 and above)
Children: $29 (ages 3–9)

Under Two Flags Island Tour
(3 hours; All ages)

As different as their European counterparts, the French and Dutch parts of this island are well worth exploring. Here's an opportunity to see the best of both worlds on a scenic narrated bus tour, which includes a stop at Marigot, the French capital, for shopping and discovering the local markets—or perhaps a coffee at a café?

What We Think *This was a good chance to see and learn about this bi-national island. Our guide was first-rate, and the air-conditioned bus was comfortable. We found the French side of the island a bit more compelling than the Dutch side; the architecture is prettier, and the restaurants are excellent—though we steered clear of the cockfighting (yikes!).*

⚓ Adults: $25 (ages 10 and above)
Children: $17 (ages 3–9)
Under age 3: free

ST. THOMAS/ST. JOHN

Among the world's most popular cruise destinations, these two islands—just 20 minutes yet a world away from each other—were discovered by Christopher Columbus in 1493, on his second journey to the New World. St. Thomas is a mere 32 square miles; St. John, its smaller sibling, is just 19 square miles.

St. Thomas has weathered its fair share of hurricane damage in the not-too-distant past but has bounced back in dramatic fashion. Rebuilt and revitalized, it has become a gathering spot for ships large, larger, and largest (some might say too many) to drop anchor. Rightfully claiming to have one of the world's most beautiful beaches, it's a destination for that alone. Yet, there is more—much more—to the island than the beach. The duty-free shopping is possibly second to none, with the streets of Charlotte Amalie overflowing with jewelry shops and galleries; it's also a place to pick up such local island souvenirs as scrimshaw, sculpture, dolls, ceramics, and basketry. Actually, you could easily spend an entire day (or days) shopping here.

A short ferry ride away, St. John is the laid-back sibling, boasting hiking trails and more than three dozen white-coral sand coves, and replete with more flowers and ferns, butterflies, and birds than would fit into the best dreamer's imaginings. As you might imagine, nature rules here, and it is a kingdom anyone—bird or human—would be proud to call their own.

St. John Eco Hike
(5 hours; Ages 6 and up)

You'll put 1.2 miles on your tennis or hiking shoes as you march through the lush forests of Cruz Bay. Scenic Lind Point Lookout and Honeymoon Beach are on the tour, too. Happily, there's plenty of time for swimming before heading to the Caneel Bay Plantation.

This gets a big thumbs-up from all of us. The scenery was amazing, the swimming superb, and the plantation was an excellent end-of-day treat.

⚓ Adults: $69 (ages 10 and above)
   Children: $50 (ages 6–9)

Magens Bay Beach Break
(4.5 hours; All ages)

Spend time enjoying the laid-back lifestyle of the Caribbean at St. Thomas's premier beach (in fact, it's considered one of the most beautiful beaches in the world), where you can swim and sunbathe (beach chairs are available on a first-come, first-served basis). Floats and water toys may be rented; beverages, snacks, and lunch items are available for purchase. Water is free. It takes about 25 minutes to get to and from the beach (via bus).

 Beach bums like us delight over this glorious day of rest and relaxation.

⚓ Adults: $47 (ages 10 and above)
Children: $37 (ages 3–9)
Under age 3: free

Doubloon Turtle Cove Sail and Snorkel Tour
(3.5 hours; Ages 5 and up)

Ahoy, matey! You'll feel as though you've stepped back in time when you board the 65-foot schooner *Doubloon*. The treasures to be found on this sail from St. Thomas are the memories you get to take home with you. And at Turtle Cove at Buck Island, you'll also have time to snorkel (equipment and beverages provided).

Note that no food is served on board, so take a snack (no fresh fruit). Our guide was meticulous in informing us about snorkeling, insisting that we wear life jackets and getting into the water with us to point out the giant sea turtles below. The captain sells souvenir Doubloon *T-shirts, so you might want to bring some cash.*

⚓ Adults: $58 (ages 10 and above)
Children: $35 (ages 5–9)

Butterfly Anytime
(All day; All ages)

Just a three-minute stroll from the pier (and your ship), this tranquil St. Thomas butterfly farm is pleasant for all ages (provided, of course, that you enjoy butterfly-watching). A friendly guide will help you discover the fascinating life cycle of the winged insect—from caterpillar to flying marvel. Don't be surprised if one of the hundreds of fluttering butterflies stops to perch on your head. And be gentle!

 Butterflies are pretty. This is our preferred way to visit them.

⚓ Adults: $12 (ages 10 and above)
Children: $6 (ages 3–9)
Under age 3: free

Screamin' Eagle Jet Boat
(1 hour; Ages 5 and up)

A 700-horsepower turbo-charged jet boat whisks guests through a scenic tour of the St. Thomas Harbor and along the coastline at breathtaking speed. Hold on tight—the 45-minute ride is anything but smooth. Guests must be at least 48 inches tall to experience the *Screamin' Eagle* jet boat.

 Very exhilarating! A real scream! Not for the faint of heart—or those wishing to stay dry.

⚓ Adults: $49 (ages 10 and above)
Children: $39 (ages 5–9)

Captain Nautica's Snorkeling Expedition
(3.5–4 hours; Ages 8 and up)

Be treated to two snorkeling spots in the gin-clear waters around St. Thomas. Board an inflatable powerboat for a 30-minute ride to picturesque Turtle Cove on Buck Island, where you'll be given snorkel, mask, fins, and a vest so you can float on the water for a dazzling look under the sea. Schools of tropical fish, parrotfish, snapper, and more inhabit the healthy reef, where you can explore for about an hour. You might even spot a sea turtle. Then it's off to Shipwreck Cove for another hour in the water with the curious fish and spectacular coral formations. Back on board, enjoy a snack as you head back to St. Thomas harbor.

 Bring along an underwater camera. The water is just 10 to 30 feet deep, so the sun reaches the coral for beautiful snapshots. And be sure to slather up with plenty of sunscreen before floating on top of the water.

⚓ Adults: $75 (ages 10 and above)
  Children: $60 (ages 8–9)

St. John Island Tour
(4–4.5 hours; All ages)

A scenic boat ride from St. Thomas brings you to the unspoiled island of St. John, where you board an open safari bus that tools around the island—including a stop at the Annaberg Ruins (with its abandoned plantation house and sugar mill)—and affords breathtaking views of neighboring islands.

What We Think — *We haven't heard great things about this tour. Most folks were wishing they were on the beach.*

⚓ Adults: $55 (ages 10 and above)
  Children: $32 (ages 9 and under)

Best of St. Thomas Island Tour and Shopping
(2.5 hours; All ages)

To fully absorb the natural beauty of the island, take this open-air (wear a hat for sun protection) safari bus ride— and be sure to bring your camera. Photo ops abound at almost every turn, especially when you reach Mountain Top, the highest point on the island.

What We Think — *If you've never been here before, this is a great way to see the sights—and it's short enough to leave time for the beach at tour's end. Kids are welcome, but little ones should sit on a grown-up's lap while on the bus.*

⚓ Adults: $39 (ages 10 and above)
  Children: $24 (ages 3–9)
  Under age 3: free

Castaway Catamaran Sail & Snorkel to Shipwreck Cove
(3–3.5 hours; Ages 5 and up)

Guests spill onto the fore-deck, sunbathe, sip a complimentary beverage, and enjoy a 40-minute sail to Shipwreck Cove. Once there, the captain drops anchor and it's fin-and-goggle-donning time. The 90-minute snorkel session takes place over a sunken shipwreck.

What We Think *We are always up for a sailing/snorkeling combo. And in this case, the shipwreck is an excellent bonus.*

⚓ Adults: $52 (ages 10 and above)
Children: $32 (ages 5–9)

SNORKELING ALERT

Snorkeling excursions are offered at most of the ports frequented by Disney Cruise Line. Olympic swimming skills aren't necessary, as all snorkelers are required to wear a snorkel vest, but guests should be comfortable in the water. Some tips:

● Before jumping in, ask the guide how much time you have and what signal to look for when it's time to return to the boat.

● The mask strap should rest above the ears (or it'll slip down the face).

● Keep hair out of the mask.

● If you can't see anything without your glasses, consider getting a prescription swimmer's mask before you leave home.

● If the mask fogs up, spit inside it. Rub the saliva around, dip it in the ocean water, and replace the mask.

● If water gets in the breathing tube, blow hard through the tube or remove the mouthpiece and empty.

● Bring an underwater camera—and wrap the strap around your wrist.

● Listen to your guide: He or she will alert you to any potential danger.

● There is a first aid kit on the boat for minor cuts and scrapes.

● Bring a towel from the Disney ship. You'll need it. (Don't forget to bring it back!)

Kayak, Hike, and Snorkel of Cas Cay
(4–4.5 hours; Ages 8 and up)

Travel by van to the Virgin Islands Eco Tours Marine Sanctuary and explore its lush, tropical ecosystem in a two-person kayak. Guests also visit a hermit crab "village" and explore a marine tidal pool and a geologic blowhole along a coral beach. The capper is a beginner-rated, guided snorkel adventure.

What We Think *If you're fit as a fiddle, this active experience can be exceptionally rewarding. The sanctuary is beautiful.*

⚓ Adults: $79 (ages 10 and above)
   Children: $59 (ages 8–9)

Coral World Ocean Park by Land and Sea
(3.5 hours; All ages)

Okay, so the semi-sub may be a mere 8 feet underwater, but the views are truly depth-defying. The adventure lasts about 45 minutes. Then you're free to spend 90 minutes exploring the marine conservation park on your own. Highlights? The Deep Reef Tank, Stingray Pool, and a three-story *underwater* observation tower.

What We Think *The park is not St. Thomas's most famous tourist attraction for nothing. If you're not claustrophobic, there are big thrills to be had.*

⚓ Adults: $56 (ages 10 and above)
   Children: $42 (ages 9 and under)

Tortola Dolphin Encounter
(8–8.5 hours; Ages 3 and up)

A one-hour ferry ride away, the island of Tortola is where you'll board a bus for an hour-long drive to Dolphin Discovery. After an orientation, each guest enjoys an in-water exchange with dolphins. Following the 30-minute meet-and-greet, a buffet-style lunch is served. Note that you will pass through immigration as you arrive and exit Tortola, so bring your passport. And the walk from the ship to the ferry is about ten minutes—be sure to wear comfortable walking shoes!

 It's a lot of traveling for a brief encounter, but all 30 minutes of dolphin-bonding are golden.

⚓ Adults: $188 (ages 10 and above)
Children: $162 (ages 3–9)

Tortola Dolphin Observer
(8–8.5 hours; Ages 3 and up)

Is a loved one taking part in the Tortola Dolphin Encounter (at left)? Would you like to tag along, take photos, learn about dolphins, and wave to the magnificent mammals from a nice, dry perch? Then this is the tour for you! Meant to be booked in conjunction with the Encounter, the Observer allows guests to accompany those participating in the Dolphin Encounter without getting wet.

What We Think *The perfect way for an aquaphobe to participate in a dolphin-y day.*

⚓ Adults: $129 (ages 10 and above)
Children: $101 (ages 3–9)

179

Sea Trek Helmet Dive at Coral World Ocean Park
(3.5 hours; Ages 10 and up)

How does a leisurely, underwater stroll sound to you? Impossible? Not here. All it takes is a Sea Trek helmet, gloves, and special water shoes (and $89)— and presto! You're ready to meander among marine life at Coral World Ocean Park—the number one tourist destination in St. Thomas. The underwater part lasts about 45 minutes and is followed by 90 minutes of free time to explore the park.

Definitely a unique underwater exploration. There is an abundance of sea life to marvel at.

⚓ Adults: $89 (ages 10 and above)

Screamin' Eagle Teens
(1–1.5 hours; Ages 14 to 17)

Take a 10-minute stroll from the ship to climb aboard the Screamin' Eagle, a 650-horse-power, turbo-charged jet boat, for a wet 'n wild ride across the ocean. The trip starts slowly as you cruise into beautiful St. Thomas harbor and your captain shares a little history. But then, hold on tight as the jet boat takes off for 30 minutes of 360-degree spins, sudden stops, and wild slides.

A safe, exhilarating getaway for teenagers, chaperoned by Disney Cruise Line youth counselors. Wear your bathing suit and flip-flops, because you will get soaked!

⚓ Teens: $49 (ages 14–17)

DISNEY'S CORPORATE CITIZENSHIP

The Walt Disney Company is focused on being responsible toward the land, sea, and all of the communities the Disney ships call home:

⚓ Every sailing, the Disney ships recycle tons of aluminum, cardboard, and plastic.

⚓ All Disney ships are painted with a special hull coating that is 100 percent nontoxic and helps increase the ship's fuel efficiency at sea.

⚓ Each ship has its own Environmental Officer dedicated to environmental training, compliance, and waste management.

⚓ Researchers at Disney's Castaway Cay are involved in a multi-year project to help rebuild healthy coral reef systems across the Bahamas. They also help to protect local marine life. For more info, visit *http://community.disneycruise.com*.

⚓ Technological enhancements and design features have been incorporated into all Disney Cruise Line ships to reduce fuel demands and increase energy efficiency.

⚓ Guests and crew members support Disney's global focus on environmental research and protection through the Disney Worldwide Conservation Fund. This fund has helped distribute more than $18 million in donations for conservation programs around the world.

⚓ Disney Cruise Line cast and crew members volunteer to clean beaches and give back in local communities, debarking the ship to clean the shore, support local schools, and help children's hospitals and care centers in ports of call. In one recent year, the DCL team generated more than 4,500 hours of community service.

COSTA MAYA

On the Yucatán Peninsula near the border of Belize in Mexico, Costa Maya is a gorgeous getaway with unspoiled jungles, pristine beaches, expansive reefs for snorkeling, and famous Mayan ruins. Built around the small seaside village of nearby Mahahual, it has been a haven for fishermen for thousands of years. Its unpaved roads, jungles, and crystal clear lagoons create a natural getaway—but the numerous restaurants, shops, pools, and bars create a bustle of activity in the center of town.

A relatively new destination for international visitors, Costa Maya's main business is tourism, with sandy beaches as abundant as they are beautiful. The most popular is Uvero Beach, with sugary sand, clear water, and charming restaurants and shops. For a dazzling peek at what's under the sea, put on a snorkel and head for the majestic Banco Chinchorro, considered to be the largest reef in Mexico and one of the biggest on the planet. Diving, too, is quite spectacular, with large blue sponges, reef fish, turtles, and sunken ships.

If you're looking for adventure and a bit of education, take a trek to Costa Maya's most famous landmark, the ruins at Chacchoben. The ruins, which were occupied from around A.D. 200 to 700, are located in a peaceful park-like setting and include magnificent stone structures and pyramids. Chacchoben remains virtually unexcavated, and you can climb the tallest pyramid and explore the lush Mayan jungle surrounding the ruins. Be sure to take a camera along for your visit!

Beach Power Snorkel

(4–4.5 hours; Ages 12 and up)

Take a 50-minute drive to one of Costa Maya's best dive and snorkel sites, where you'll learn how to operate a Sea-Doo Scooter and snorkel equipment with a certified dive master. Glide along the gorgeous reef for 50 minutes, passing sea fans, coral, and marine life. Wrap up with time to relax or play for an hour on the private beach.

 What We Think *So much fun to glide along on the water scooter faster than you can swim!*

⚓ Adults: $55 (ages 12 and up)

Dolphin Swim

(1–1.5 hours; Ages 8 and up)

Walk from the ship to the pier, where you meet the friendly, intelligent marine mammals during a 30-minute interaction when you can hug and touch the dolphins, and learn how they are trained. Then jump in for a thrilling ride through the water as you hold on to their pectoral fins. (Kids ages 8 to 12 need to swim with a paying adult.)

What We Think *Swimming with dolphins is a magical, memorable experience for any age.*

⚓ Adults: $119 (ages 10 and above)
   Children: $99 (ages 8–9)

The Mayans Through the Ages
(4–4.5 hours; All ages)

If you think the Mayan civilization disappeared a long time ago, this tour will show you that their way of life is alive and well—the culture, customs, language, and beliefs continue on the Yucatán Peninsula. You'll travel 45 minutes by bus to a town where most locals descended from the ancient Maya, with a stop at the ruins of a Mayan site. Next, visit a home to learn about local food, ancient medicines, history, legends, and Mayan culture, followed by a traditional Mayan lunch.

 Fascinating immersion in a centuries-old culture—and the delicious lunch includes favorites like guacamole, salsa, and tortillas.

⚓ Adults: $85 (ages 10 and above)
Children: $65 (ages 3–9)
Under age 3: free

Bike & Clear-Bottom Kayak
(3–3.5 hours; Ages 10 and up)

Take off on your bicycle from the pier and ride south for about 30 minutes to the sleepy fishing village of Mahahual, where your kayaking experience begins. You'll get gorgeous views of the coral reef and marine life through the glass bottom of the two-person kayak as you paddle for about an hour. A leisurely bike ride back to the pier takes you along beautiful stretches of sand.

Burn off energy in this fun outing that takes you along breathtaking coastline, then out to the blue waters of the Caribbean.

⚓ Adults: $59 (Ages 10 and above)

Costa Maya Salsa & Salsa
(2.5–3 hours; Ages 6 and up)

Take a short shuttle ride to a beachfront restaurant, where you'll learn how to make three authentic salsas in a hands-on cooking class. Next, mix and sip margaritas before hitting the dance floor for another kind of salsa—Latin America's most lively dance. While you learn the basics, the kids have fun at their own piñata party. Cap off your "salsa & salsa" getaway with a cool splash in the ocean.

What We Think — *Food is the heart and dance is the soul of any culture, and this happy excursion gives you a taste of both.*

⚓ Adults: $65 (ages 10 and above)
   Children: $45 (ages 6–9)

Chacchoben Mayan Ruins
(4–4.5 hours; All ages)

Learn about the Yucatán Peninsula as you travel an hour by bus to Chacchoben Mayan Ruins, which means "place of red corn" in Mayan. You'll have plenty of time to explore these sacred temples, thought to have been constructed between 300 and 500 A.D., as you hear the fascinating history of the Mayans. Mahogany trees, giant palms, and enormous banyan trees create a picturesque backdrop.

What We Think — *These majestic temple pyramids are a calm, peaceful place to spend a few hours. Wear comfortable shoes; you'll be walking a lot, including climbing stairs.*

⚓ Adults: $75 (ages 10 and above)
   Children: $59 (ages 3–9)
   Under age 3: free

Discover Scuba Diving

(3.5–4 hours; Ages 12 and up)

If you're up for a real adventure, head to the dive center in the sleepy town of Mahahual and suit up for a fascinating peek under the sea. Experts will give you a 45-minute introductory lesson to scuba—no certification required. You'll board the dive boat for a short ride out to the magnificent Mesoamerican Barrier Reef, one of the largest reef systems in the world that's known for its beautiful corals and exotic marine life—turtles, lobsters, stingrays, sea horses, and a nearly endless variety of tropical reef fish. Serious divers head here for some of the world's best scuba, and virtually anyone who is in good health, reasonably fit, and comfortable in the water can experience these hidden treasures beneath the turquoise waters of the Caribbean.

It's exciting to learn to scuba, then dive some of the world's most spectacular reefs.

⚓ Adults: $125 (ages 12 and above)

JUNEAU

Chances are that if your family and friends haven't taken a cruise up here, they haven't been to Juneau. This area is as remote as it gets! This "city"—which sits at the base of the majestic Mount Juneau amid a rainforest—is the largest U.S. state capital and the only one that is accessible by air or ship only.

Juneau is at the northern end of the Inside Passage. Here, in addition to scenery to die for, visitors can take a walking tour of places such as the State Capitol (there's not much to see unless the legislature is in session—but you can say you've been there!), the Governor's Mansion, and the State Office Building, home to the Alaska State Museum (it has, among other super-cool stuff, hand-painted totems), and Centennial Hall. Of course, there's much more to do here than sightsee.

Take some steps back in time and sign up for a gold mine tour, and be sure to watch salmon swim at the Macaulay Salmon Hatchery. And if you really love fish—not just watching or catching them, but devouring 'em— you've come to the right place. Once you've sampled fresh Pacific salmon here at the source, everything you've had back home will pale by comparison.

Here are some other neat experiences that guests may pack into a jaunt in Juneau: go *flightseeing* over the ice fields, discover dogsledding, take a boat tour for some humpback whale-watching, grab a camera for a scenery-rich ride on the Mount Roberts Tramway, and take a bus tour to the Mendenhall Glacier. Awesome is an understatement when describing this port of call.

Enchanted Taku Glacier Lodge Flight and Feast

(3.5–4 hours; Ages 2 and up)

Take a thrilling 30-minute flight in a nostalgic floatplane over five glaciers, the deep blue crevasses of the Juneau Icefield, snow-capped mountains, waterfalls, and lush forests. You'll land near the historic Taku Lodge, built in 1923, on the Taku River and directly across from the Hole-In-The-Wall Glacier, one of the few advancing glaciers in Alaska. Start your lodge experience with fresh wild Alaska king salmon for lunch while a host regales guests with colorful stories. The storytelling continues after lunch with Alaska pioneer character Mary Joyce, who brings history to life. Then you can take a stroll on your own or head out with a nature guide—you might just see a black bear!

The flight is fantastic, and everyone gets a window seat. Best for ages 5 and older. It's expensive—but for some it's the adventure of a lifetime. Hard to put a price on that!

⚓ Adults: $309 (ages 10 and above)
   Children: $265 (ages 2–9)

Disney Exclusive: Glacier Dog Musher for a Day
(4–4.5 hours; Ages 5 and up)

This adventure kicks off with a 20-minute helicopter ride over the Juneau Icefield. The chopper touches down in a region accessible only by air. Green forests, alpine lakes, snow-capped mountains, and glaciers form a stunning backdrop. Then the fun begins as you meet the sled dogs of the famous Iditarod and see where they live, then head out across the snow-capped glacier for the ride of a lifetime.

What We Think *Fantastic experience for youngsters, from the helicopter ride to a day with the dogs. Dress warmly and wear comfortable shoes.*

⚓ Adults: $709 (ages 10 and above)
Children: $499 (ages 5–9)

Alaska Salmon Bake, Glacier, & Hatchery
(4.5–5 hours; All ages)

Venture out to Mendenhall Valley by motor coach (about 25 minutes) to Alaska's only glacier that is accessible by road. The area has wilderness trails, view-points of the glacier, and places to see sockeye salmon running in late July and August. Then travel a short distance to Macaulay Salmon Hatchery to learn about salmon and Alaska's fishing industry (with touch tanks the kids are sure to love). The fun ends with an old-fashioned salmon bake.

What We Think *Glacier geeks will love the Mendenhall Glacier Visitor Center, with all sorts of interactive displays. And dinner is delicious.*

⚓ Adults: $90 (ages 10 and above)
Children: $60 (ages 3–9)
Under age 3: free

Best of Juneau
(6–6.5 hours; All ages)

Set sail on a catamaran for guaranteed whale watching with a spectacular backdrop of snow-capped peaks and glaciers. In addition to humpback and/or killer whales, you might also catch a glimpse of seals, porpoises, sea lions, bald eagles, bears, and deer. For lunch, enjoy a feast at Orca Point Lodge on Colt Island. The menu includes grilled, wild Alaska salmon (of course!). The day is capped off with a short drive to Mendenhall Glacier.

What We Think *We love the catamaran's warm, spacious indoor cabin with large windows. And you get a $100 refund if you don't see a whale (but they haven't had to give a refund in at least 10 years).*

⚓ Adults: $199 (ages 10 and above)
   Children: $122 (ages 9 and under)

Exclusive Whale Encounter & Mendenhall Glacier
(4–4.5 hours; All ages)

Just 36 lucky folks at a time get to climb aboard a boat in Auke Bay to head out to sea. Be on the look-out for whales, porpoises, sea lions, seals, and bald eagles. Each boat has an underwater microphone to hear the song of the whales—and there's a money-back guarantee if you don't spot one. Taste wild Alaskan salmon, Alaskan chocolate, and other goodies while you cruise. The day comes to a dramatic conclusion with a visit to Mendenhall Glacier.

What We Think *Cruising on the small boat is fast and fun, and it's quiet enough (no propeller) for marine mammals to safely swim nearby.*

⚓ Adults: $139 (ages 10 and above)
   Children: $89 (ages 9 and under)

Fins and Grins
(3–3.5 hours; Ages 6 and up)

Board a 30-foot cabin cruiser (6 guests ride at a time) in Auke Bay and set out for the fishing trip of a lifetime. You might see eagles, deer, and bears as you parallel the scenic tidelands of Gastineau Channel on your journey. Cast a line for cod, flounder, sole, herring, and sculpin (and occasional salmon and halibut), all caught in these waters. Though it might be hard to concentrate on your fishing skills with whales, sea lions, harbor seals, and porpoises frolicking in the waters and the gorgeous Mendenhall Glacier in view! Dress warmly and take along rain gear for a day on the water. Note that guests ages 16 and older are required to pay $20 for a fishing license and $10 for a king salmon stamp. (If you manage to catch one, you can have it shipped home!) Payment must be made in cash. Snacks are served on the way back to the dock (PB&J sandwiches, smoked salmon, crackers, and bottled water).

A great day for wildlife lovers. Keep your camera, binoculars, and a jacket handy at all times. It can get quite chilly.

⚓ Adults: $219 (ages 10 and above)
  Children: $189 (ages 6–9)

Dog Sled Summer Camp
(2–2.5 hours; All ages)

Head out along Gastineau Channel to remote, gorgeous Sheep Creek Valley, where you're greeted by professional mushers and teams of Alaskan huskies. Start with a tour of the Sheep Creek Summer Dog Camp (on the site of a famous gold mine with tales of the Gold Rush days), then see a replica of an Iditarod race checkpoint and learn just what it takes to be a musher in the world's foremost sled race. Best of all, you get to cuddle with the adorable husky pups! Then climb aboard a specially designed wheeled sled made for seasons without snow for a ride through the valley for about 15 minutes, surrounded by magnificent scenery. Back at camp, you'll get one more chance to snuggle with the puppies before you return to the ship.

Learn what it's like to live in the middle of 120 happy Alaskan huskies. Dog lovers especially enjoy this outing.

⚓ Adults: $154 (ages 10 and above)
Children: $142 (ages 3–9)
Under age 3: free

Whale Quest & Orca Point Lodge
(5–5.5 hours; All ages)

You're guaranteed to see a whale on this adventure, centered around a memorable 2½-hour cruise. Head to Auke Bay by motor coach, where you'll board a spacious catamaran designed for viewing wildlife (the warm main cabin features extra-large windows). Sail though the island-studded waters of Stephen's Passage with snow-capped peaks and glaciers as the backdrop, keeping an eye out for humpback and killer whales, sea lions, porpoises, seals, bald eagles, bears and deer. A naturalist is onboard to explain the behavior and habitat of wildlife you may encounter. Step ashore at secluded Orca Point Lodge on Colt Island for an hour-long lunch including grilled wild Alaska salmon, then stroll along the beach before heading back.

If you want to see a whale, this is your chance—they're so sure you'll spot one that you get a $100 cash refund if you don't.

⚓ Adults: $168 (ages 10 and above)
    Children: $100 (ages 9 and under)

KETCHIKAN

Welcome to the world of whales and other wondrous sights, Alaska's self-proclaimed salmon capital of the world. Here in the wilderness, adventure awaits. But before we venture into the forests primeval, here's a bit of background: This region is part of the Alaska panhandle and was first noticed by Europeans in 1793. That's when George Vancouver discovered New Eddystone Rock. Said "rock" is really a 237-foot-tall column of basalt (volcanic rock) formed within the past 5 million years. It's now part of Misty Fjords National Monument.

Ketchikan is located on Revillogigedo Island, 235 miles south of Juneau (see page 189). The average summer temperature here ranges from about 46 to 66 degrees (Fahrenheit).

Among its famous attractions is the aforementioned, fog-shrouded Misty Fjords National Monument. Its towering cliffs and waterfalls can be enjoyed by air (tours can be arranged on a float-plane); from these heights you may well spot a bear or even a whale.

For the slightly more daring travelers, kayaking adventures await you, bringing you up close and personal with many of nature's lesser-known sights. Here, too, you will find the world's largest collection of totem poles.

For a cerebral experience, you can seek out the museums and art galleries along the Ketchikan Creek. And for just plain fun, don't return to your ship without seeing the Great Alaskan Lumberjack Show, where hardy woodsmen compete against each other in spirited log-rolling and tree-climbing contests. Fun for everyone!

Disney Exclusive: Bering Sea Crab Fisherman's Tour and Dinner with the Crew

(5–5.5 hours; Ages 8 and up)

After a short stroll from the ship, you'll board the *Aleutian Ballad* and cast off with skilled Bering Sea crab fishermen. Beautiful scenery all along the way—keep an eye out for whales, sea lions, and seals. A true highlight is watching the fishermen haul in 700-pound king crab pots, with everything placed in an on-deck aquarium for a close-up view. (You might even want to hold some of these strange sea creatures.) Other catches include octopus, eels, giant Dungeness crab, and shrimp. End the day at a local restaurant in Ketchikan for a crab feast, where a member of the crew will share stories of life on the Bering Sea.

This trip includes 3 hours at sea. That is a bit much for many landlubbers, but if you've got the stamina—and the sea legs—it's an amazing day.

⚓ Adults: $265 (ages 10 and above)
  Children: $159 (ages 8–9)

Disney Exclusive: The Great Alaskan Lumberjack Enhanced Show

(1–1.5 hours; Ages 3 and up)

A few steps (and a world away) from the ship, you will experience a 90-minute, action-packed show starring some of the world's top timber sport athletes (you might have actually seen these guys on ESPN and the Outdoor Channel). Jaws drop as these guys wield axes and saws (and chain saws!) and compete in the death-defying speed climb, log rolling, and all sorts of cool stunts. Who's going to win the title "Bull of the Woods"? You have to be here to find out. You'll pick up a little history of the timber industry in Alaska, too. Afterward, guests are encouraged to stick around for autographs and photos with the stars of the show.

> **What We Think** *Parts of this show are just for Disney Cruise Line guests. How cool is that? And it's a perfect excursion on a rainy day—the grandstand is covered.*

⚓ Adults: $40 (ages 10 and above)
Children: $19 (ages 3–9)

Totems, Exclusive Lumberjack Show & Potlatch Park
(4–4.5 hours; Ages 5 and up)

Following a 20-minute motor coach ride to Totem Bight State Park, you'll get close-up views of real totem poles and learn about southeast Alaska's flora and fauna on a beautiful nature trail. Next, you will visit a re-created native settlement at Potlatch Park. Highlights here include a Tribal House, a salmon smoke shack, and a lesson about totem carving. (Kids get to paint their very own wooden feather that will be added to a totem pole just for Disney Cruise Line guests.) And everyone gets a hand-carved totem pole to take home. Finish up the day at the action-packed Great Alaskan Lumberjack Show (see page 199).

This hands-on history lesson is for all ages. And we love that they have a Disney Cruise Line totem pole!

⚓ Adults: $127 (ages 10 and above)
    Children: $97 (ages 5–9)

Alaska Coastal Expedition
(4–4.5 hours; Ages 10 and up)

After a short walk from ship to shore, guests board a 15-foot motorized inflatable boat with three other adventure-seekers (you must be at least 25 years old to drive) and take off on a two-hour search for bears, eagles, seals, whales, and other wild animals in hard-to-reach places. From the boat, you'll see Saxman Native Village and George Inlet Cannery and learn a bit of history, to boot. Before heading back to the ship, you'll take a break at a wilderness camp and remote beach (a warm beverage and snack are provided, as are breathtaking views). Be sure to dress warmly—this *is* Alaska!

For fit adventure seekers—you need to be in pretty good shape to keep up. If you are uncomfortable with motion or being exposed to weather, sit this one out.

⚓ Adults and children: $159 (ages 10 and above)

Bear Country & Wildlife Expedition
(3–3.5 hours; Ages 5 and up)

Offered from mid-July through September, this is a chance to search for black bears on a guided walk with just 12 guests. You'll head out to the Alaska Rainforest Sanctuary where there are five suspension bridges and seven platforms for close (and safe!) bear viewing. Spend an hour and a half on the trail, walking at a leisurely pace, though you may need to move quickly if wildlife is sighted. An elevated boardwalk continues above Eagle Creek and alongside Whitman Hatchery, home to major runs of Pacific salmon in the summertime. You'll end with a chance to photograph and feed Alaskan reindeer, a visit to the Alaska Wildlife Foundation's raptor center, and time with a master totem carver.

A portion of the trail is on elevated walkways 10 to 25 feet off the ground—so if you're got a fear of heights, beware.

⚓ Adults: $192 (ages 10 and above)
Children: $129 (ages 5–9)

The Best of Ketchikan: Land and Sea
(3.5–4 hours; All ages)

Head out via motor coach to Saxman Village for a close-up look at one of the world's largest collection of totem poles, where the guide will interpret the meanings of these giant sentries. Next up, an easy stroll through the rainforest at George Inlet to historic Libby Cannery, where you'll hear stories of the harvesting and processing of salmon, including a look at the Tsirku Canning Line, the only functioning equipment of its kind in the world. From there, board a water jet-powered vessel with a naturalist to explore the inlet's glacier-carved coastline—keep an eye out for eagles, seals, porpoises, and other wildlife. The tour ends as you enter Tongass Narrows for a view of Ketchikan, Alaska's busiest port and "salmon capital of the world."

A great day for wildlife lovers. Keep your camera and binoculars handy at all times. And bundle up—it can get quite chilly.

⚓ Adults: $125 (ages 10 and above)
   Children: $189 (ages 3–9)
   Under age 3: $75

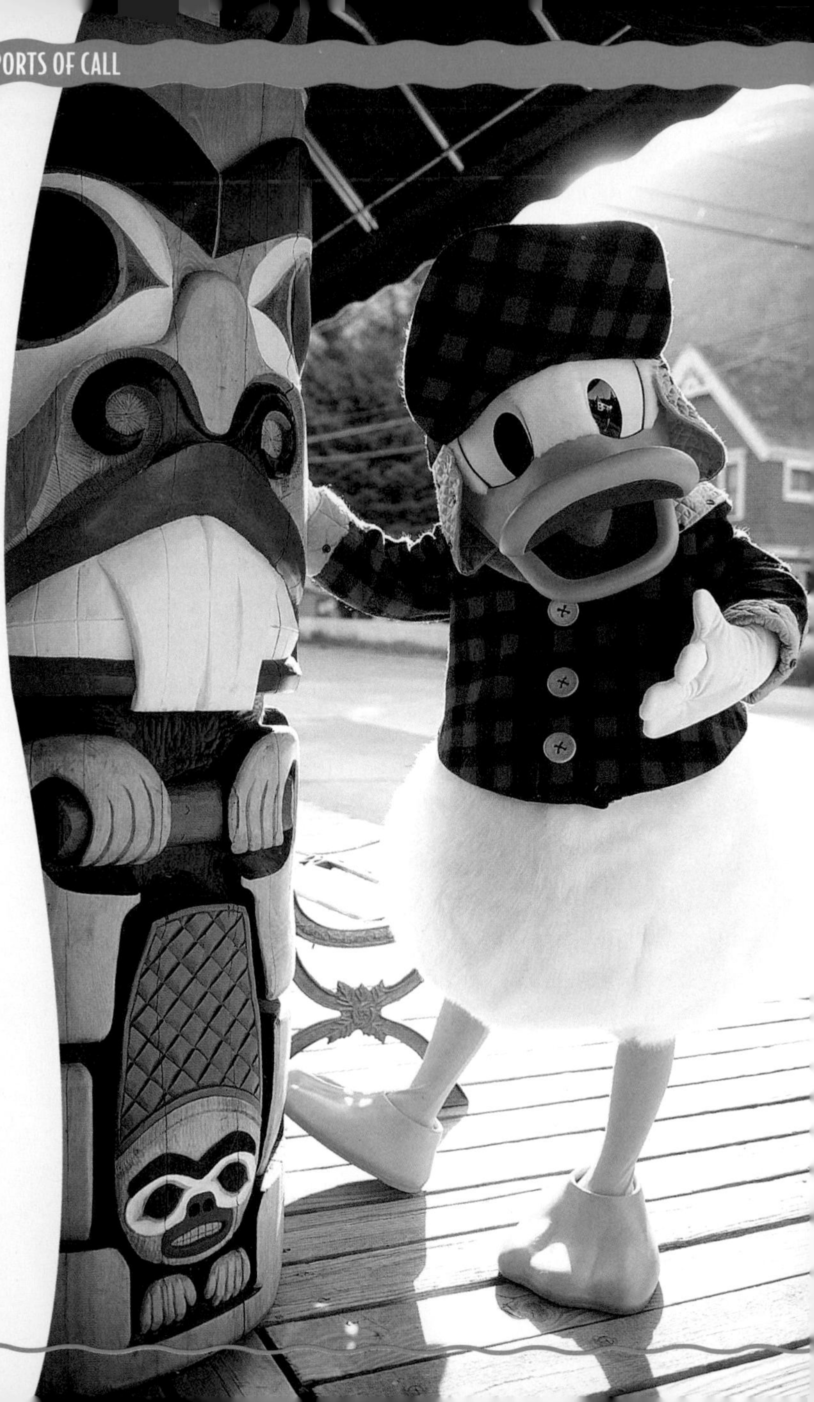

SKAGWAY

Now that you're almost at the top of the world—or at least the top of the United States—take a moment to soak up the sights and sounds of the scenic Borough of Skagway. This haven's winter population is a mere 862, but in season, when cruise passengers like yourselves flock here, that number soars to approximately one million.

First a bit of history: The name Skagway in its original Tlingit form (the language of the area's indigenous people) is *Skgagwei*. It's meaning? Windy places with caps on the water. The borough's stock in trade is you: Tourism brings some serious bucks to the local economy. In fact, the White Pass and Yukon River railroad (once a vital part of the area's mining past) now chugs along exclusively for the benefit of cruise passengers and operates only during the summer months.

This neck of the woods was a lot more bustling back in 1896, when gold was discovered in the Klondike region. Thousands upon thousands of King Midas wannabes flocked to Skagway by sea, preparing themselves for the arduous 500-mile journey to the gold mines.

Thanks to the gold rush, this sleepy little town then became the largest city in Alaska—though it is now one of the smallest "cities" in the state. (Anchorage is currently top dog when it comes to population.) Today's visitors will find the above-mentioned railway, hiking trails galore, and quaint shops selling gold-mine-related souvenirs. Though you are unlikely to strike it rich, your memories of this place will certainly be golden.

Liarsville Gold Rush Trail Camp & Salmon Bake
(2.5–3 hours; All ages)

Board a motor coach for Skagway's historic downtown, then head out to Liarsville Gold Rush Trail Camp and Salmon Bake. There, a cast of "sourdoughs" (a sourdough is a person who has lived in Alaska for at least one winter, often a pioneer or a prospector) and dance hall girls will entertain you with a funny puppet show highlighting tales of the gold rush era. You'll learn about gold panning, then search for treasure with Disney characters. You're guaranteed to find gold in every pan! Finish with a fabulous feast of wild Alaskan salmon, chicken, pasta, and other goodies. Finally, you'll enjoy toasting marshmallows around a campfire and posing for photos with your favorite Disney characters.

Lots of fun for the whole family—and terrific photo opportunities with the Disney characters. The best of both worlds (those being Disney's and the real world).

⚓ Adults: $89 (ages 10 and above)
Children: $49 (ages 3–9)
Under age 3: free

Musher's Camp & Sled Dog Experience
(3–3.5 hours; All ages)

It's a 40-minute ride to the Klondike Gold Rush National Historical Park and the Musher's Camp, where you'll board vehicles for some off-road fun. Then you'll meet the dogs that will pull you on a wheeled sled—custom made for running during the snowless summer months. The husky team will whisk you along a one-mile trail through a temperate rainforest. Take time to visit with the dogs and their precious puppies.

 A true Alaskan adventure. It's fun for kids to meet the dog musher and learn about the sport (and to cuddle with the puppies).

⚓ Adults: $132 (ages 10 and above)
　Children: $125 (ages 3–9)
　Under age 3: free

All Aboard Steam Train
(4–4.5 hours; All ages)

Choo-choo! Board a vintage rail car and an authentic steam engine will take you for a 4-hour, fully narrated journey through the historic White Pass & Yukon Route. Follow the trail of the Klondike Gold Rush up one of the steepest grades in North America, then raise a toast at the summit and receive a numbered brass ornament certifying you're part of the "White Pass Summit Club."

Marvelling at gorgeous mountains, glaciers, and waterfalls—all from the comfort of a vintage rail car? Pretty unforgettable.

⚓ Adults: $214 (ages 10 and above)
　Children: $105 (ages 3–9)
　Under age 3: free

Best of Skagway
(6.5–7 hours; Ages 16 and up)

A vintage rail car takes you through the historic White Pass and Yukon Route, an engineering wonder climbing nearly 3,000 feet over cliff-hanging turns. Arrive in British Columbia and travel by motor coach down the spectacular Klondike Highway, stopping for a salmon bake lunch at Liarsville Gold Rush Trail Camp, where you'll learn how to pan for gold. Then it's hilarious live entertainment with a cast of "sourdoughs" (folks who have lived in Alaska for at least one winter—often an old prospector or a pioneer) and dance hall girls. End at the famous Red Onion Saloon, where you can enjoy an Alaskan amber beer, wine, or root beer as you hear tales about the historic building.

Lots of travel time and grown-up entertainment. Take your passport; the tour crosses the Canadian border.

⚓ Adults and children: $220 (ages 16 and above)

Alaska Nature & Wildlife Expedition
(6–6.5 hours; Ages 5 and up)

Hop aboard a catamaran for a 45-minute cruise down the glacial fjord between Skagway and Haines. In Haines, you'll board a bus and head to a special location for seasonal wildlife viewing in the ocean, estuary, river, lake, forest, and swamp. Binoculars and powerful spotting scopes add to the fun as you look for mountain goats, bears, bald eagles, birds, and waterfowl. A fish technician shows how they count and sample salmon—part of the leisurely day of exploration and observation of animal behavior. Enjoy a picnic-style lunch with a naturalist/guide who will be happy to answer any and all questions. Although children as young as age 5 may partake in this port adventure, it is best enjoyed by kids ages 10 and up.

Mother Nature at her stunning best! And fantastic photo opportunities of wildlife in natural habitats.

⚓ Adults: $168 (ages 10 and above)
 Children: $114 (ages 5–9)

Sunset Horseback Adventure
(3–3.5 hours; Ages 12 and up; minimum height of 58 inches)

Drive along the seaside through historic Skagway for about 30 minutes and out to a ranch in historic Dyea, where you'll saddle up and head into Klondike Gold Rush National Historic Park for about an hour and 45 minutes on horseback. It's such a pretty journey—the guides stop halfway through to snap photos of you and your horse with the ocean as a backdrop, and they share lots of stories about Dyea and its days as a trading boomtown during the gold rush. As you traverse the park, you'll be able to see how millions of years of titanic forces have shaped the rugged landscape. And if all that fresh air makes you hungry, you can get a taste of Alaskan cooking such as roasted salmon as you relax around a campfire back at the ranch.

Gentle horses, an easy walk, and a nice way to enjoy the magnificent scenery: snow-capped mountains, streams, wildflowers. You may even spot an eagle or other wildlife.

⚓ Adults: $210 (ages 12 and above)

White Pass Scenic Railway Featuring Exclusive Youth Activity

(3.5–4 hours; Ages 5 and up)

A vintage rail car comes right to the pier to pick you up for a trip along Alaska's historic White Pass & Yukon Route. This engineering wonder climbs nearly 3,000 feet over 20 miles of steep grades and cliff-hanging turns—a trail carved in 1898 through some of the North's most rugged terrain. You'll pass iconic spots such as Bridal Veil Falls, Inspiration Point, and Dead Horse Gulch as you chug along the original route to the White Pass Summit. Once you're at the summit, kids ages 5 to 9 have their very own train car for the journey back, with games and stories of the gold rush. And grown-ups get a champagne or sparkling cider toast and a holiday ornament to welcome them into the "White Pass Summit Club."

It's a fun history lesson for all ages. Let the kids head to their own train car for the trip back down the mountain—a Disney Youth counselor will be with them at all times.

⚓ Adults: $169 (ages 10 and above)
   Children: $99 (ages 5–9)

VICTORIA

"Quaint and charming with more than a touch of Great Britain" just begins to describe this provincial capital of British Columbia, named after Queen Victoria. Its Victorian architecture, spacious parks, manicured gardens, and friendly people (many of British descent) all enhance this harbor city's appeal. Double-decker buses add to the already British flavor of this locale.

Thousands of years before any European set foot on the North American continent, the island's natives used deer antlers to chop down trees to build homes and canoes. Superstition of those days held that the condor created thunder by fluttering its wings and made lightning bolts with a flash of its eyes.

Totem poles and other carvings of the powerful bird can be seen at the British Columbia Museum. (We hope that legendary condor will not flutter its wings to mar your sun-filled vacation!)

Victoria offers visual and intellectual adventures: Look around you—ocean, gardens, and mountains are all yours for the gratis gazing. There's also a wealth of history here: The Art Gallery of Greater Victoria, one of Canada's finest art museums, is home to North America's only Shinto shrine. And Thunderbird Park is totem pole central. Shopping, hiking, whale watching, biking, and fishing are available here, too. But above all, do not leave the area without visiting the flowery magnificence that is Butchart Gardens.

Victoria's not just one of *our* favorite places—mention it to *anyone* who has been there and they will surely bond with you over the beauty of this scenic city.

Afternoon Tea at Butchart Gardens
(4–4.5 hours; Ages 8 and up)

Take a scenic drive, then a relaxing stroll through beautiful Butchart Gardens, a National Historic Site of Canada. See how Jennie Butchart transformed a quarry site into a 55-acre jewel that is considered one of the world's top horticultural attractions (still privately owned). Relax and enjoy gracious, traditional tea service in the best Victorian style in the main dining room, where petit fours, house-made sweets, salads, and sandwiches create an elegant repast.

One of the prettiest places in the world. It's about 1.5 miles of walking, so wear comfortable shoes!

⚓ Adults: $135 (ages 10 and above)
   Children: $109 (ages 8–9)

Creatures of the Air & Sea
(4–4.5 hours; All ages)

Start this adventure at Victoria Butterfly Gardens, strolling for an hour through the warm atmosphere and learning about the life of a butterfly—many will flutter by! Next, visit the Shaw Ocean Discovery Centre, with its touch pools and other hands-on activities that focus on colorful life under the Salish Sea.

 Butterfly Garden is an explosion of color—it is pretty as a picture. Do bring a camera.

⚓ Adults: $79 (ages 10 and above)
Children: $45 (ages 9 and under)

Horse-Drawn Trolley Tour
(1–1.5 hours; All ages)

The tour vehicle, an open-sided horse-drawn trolley, is pulled by two majestic Percheron or Clydesdale horses. As scenic tours go, this one is exceptionally picturesque—the hour-long ride takes guests past the Olympic Mountain Range, through one of the city's original neighborhoods, and offers views of Beacon Hill Park and the Inner Harbour.

 A leisurely way to see the city. The trolley seats up to 20, so it's a group experience.

⚓ Adults: $59 (ages 10 and above)
Children: $42 (ages 3–9)
Under age 3: free

215

Ocean Wildlife & Orca Expedition
(3–3.5 hours; All ages)

A high-speed catamaran or a single-hulled vessel will take you out to sea in search of wildlife on this port adventure. Sightings may include seals, porpoise, dolphins, and even orcas (whales). You also may see eagles, great blue herons, and many other water birds. The waters around Vancouver Island are home to the distinctive black-and-white orcas, though a sighting is not guaranteed (they travel up to 100 miles in a day in any direction!).

The sight of these magnificent sea creatures will take your breath away. So humbling. Obviously, great photo ops abound. You're on the water for more than two hours, so dress warmly in layers—and carry rain gear.

⚓ Adults: $142 (ages 10 and above)
Children: $92 (ages 9 and under)

Waterfront Walking Tour
(1–1.5 hours; All ages)

Begin your stroll at the dock and head to pretty downtown Victoria (about one mile) with your first stop at the quaint Fisherman's Wharf, where you can observe all the activity—and, if you're lucky, the seals may be visiting. Walk on to the Visitor Centre, with stories and stops along the way.

 What We Think *Stick around for shopping. A shuttle ticket is provided so you can return to the pier at your leisure.*

⚓ Adults: $40 (ages 10 and above)
Children: $32 (ages 9 and under)

HOLIDAY CRUISES

On special sailings, usually during the Christmas holidays, Disney Cruise Line adds a couple of destinations to its cruises. The trade-off (there always is one) is that you may have to sacrifice two of those leisurely sea days. But if these ports appeal to you, remember: These extra-special sailings only happen once or twice a year. Check with your travel agent for dates. Know that special cruises are very popular and tend to sell out far in advance. For information on upcoming special sailings, visit *www.disneycruise.com*, or call 800-910-3659.

LAND AND SEA VACATIONS
Pairing a Disney Cruise with a Walt Disney World Vacation

It's the ultimate surf-and-turf experience for Disney fans—a Walt Disney World vacation that's paired with a Disney Cruise. (What better way to chase the Pirates of the Caribbean attraction than by visiting the Caribbean?! Sans real pirates, of course.) And, with the addition of the Dream and the Fantasy to the fleet, "land and sea" opportunities are limitless. The chapter that follows describes how Land and Sea vacations work and gives a brief overview of Walt Disney World accommodations and attractions. (We will resist the temptation to overwhelm you with details here. For more info on WDW, check out *Birnbaum's Official Guide to Walt Disney World 2014*.)

If you've been to Disney's world before, you know that it is not a small one. In fact, it covers 40 square miles— and with about as many attractions, restaurants, and places to stay as one might expect from an area that size. There are four theme parks, two water parks, two dozen hotels, a dining, shopping, and entertainment district, championship golf courses, boating, fishing, tennis, and more. Add a cruise to the mix, and even seasoned Disney veterans run the risk of becoming overwhelmed.

The good news is that a customized vacation package can include just about everything you'd ever want. That frees you up to focus on an important goal: having fun.

Land and Sea Vacations

One of the most popular ways to enjoy a Disney vacation, this experience combines a stay at a Walt Disney World resort with a cruise aboard one of the four ships in Disney Cruise Line's fleet. While land-sea "packages" are not offered, it's easy to pair a visit to Walt Disney World with a Disney cruise; just call 800-951-3532. (That's the number to call if you'd like help finding a hotel near Disney Cruise Line's other home ports, too.)

Whether you do the land part of your vacation before or after the sea leg, you will have a choice of Walt Disney World's wide variety of themed resort hotels.

If you have cruise-related questions while at Walt Disney World, know there is a Cruise Line information desk in many Disney resorts. Check with the lobby concierge for specifics.

DISNEY CRUISE LINE AIR PROGRAM

If you plan to fly to the port, consider allowing the Disney Cruise Vacations Air Program to help you make the arrangements. In addition to lining up round-trip airfare for your whole party, they will secure motor coach ground transportation and baggage transfers. The service is available in more than 150 cities in the United States, United Kingdom, and Canada. For details, call 877-566-0967. At press time, this service was not included in the price of any of the vacation packages.

WHAT'S INCLUDED? WHAT'S NOT?

Walt Disney World/Disney Cruise Line combination vacations can include accommodations on land (at a WDW resort) and a stateroom on a Disney ship. In addition to accommodations, shipboard meals, snacks, soft drinks, and entertainment are included with all Disney Cruise Line packages.

What's not included in a "Land and Sea" combination vacation? Meals and beverages at Walt Disney World (unless the WDW Dining Plan is purchased in advance), transfers to Port Canaveral (although these may also be purchased in advance), airfare, excursions, meals ashore in ports of call (with the exception of Castaway Cay), extra gratuities, laundry or valet services, parking at the port, or any other items not specifically included.

What can be added? Just about everything. Options include tickets to Disney World theme and water parks, dinner shows, and more. For details, visit *www.disneycruise.com*, or call 800-951-3532.

☀ HOT TIP

Disney Cruise Vacations offers a day-before option at a non-Disney resort with some packages. For information, contact a travel agent or call 800-951-3532.

Walt Disney World Resorts

All of the 20-plus Walt Disney World properties hold the promise of partnering with a Disney Cruise Line voyage. (For a complete listing, turn to page 228.) We've stayed at all of them and can vouch for each and every one. What follows is a sampling of resorts from which you can choose. (For details on WDW resorts, visit *www.disneyworld.com*, or grab a copy of *Birnbaum's Official Guide to Walt Disney World 2014*.)

Animal Kingdom Lodge

The zebras, ostriches, and Thomson's gazelles out back are not escapees from the nearby Animal Kingdom theme park. They and their hoofed and feathered comrades live on the resort's carefully plotted pasturelands, giving round-the-clock credence to its claim as Florida's only African wildlife reserve lodge.

Romance and adventure cling to every richly appointed inch of the semicircular lodge, which serves as a five-story animal observation platform and boasts animal-viewing parlors, stellar restaurants, and an expansive swimming pool.

LOCATION: Animal Kingdom area
BIG DRAWS: Luxury laced with an undeniable spirit of adventure and romance. Amazing animal views from most resort rooms.

Beach Club

This setting conjures up such a heady vision of turn-of-the-century Nantucket and Martha's Vineyard, you'd swear you smelled salt in the air. Surely, architect Robert A. M. Stern's evocation of the grand old seaside hotels has the gulls fooled. The resort stretches along a picturesque shoreline, complete with a swimming lagoon, lighthouse, and marina.

LOCATION: Epcot area
BIG DRAWS: The exceptional swimming area is second to none. Some of the World's best restaurants. Easy access to Epcot and Disney's Hollywood Studios.

IMPORTANT WDW TELEPHONE NUMBERS

- Walt Disney World Information:
  407-824-4321

- Special Reservations Department (for guests with special needs):
  407-939-7807 (voice);
  407-939-7670 (TTY)

- Recreation: 407-WDW-PLAY (939-7529)

- Dining Reservations:
  407-WDW-DINE (939-3463)

- Centra Care Walk-In Urgent Care:
  407-934-2273

- Children's Activity Centers:
  407-939-3463

Caribbean Beach Resort

In this colorful evocation of the Caribbean, the spirit of the islands is captured by a lake ringed by beaches and villages representing Barbados, Martinique, Trinidad, Jamaica, and Aruba. Each village is marked by clusters of two-story buildings that transport you to the Caribbean, with cool pastel facades, white railings, and metallic roofs. Old Port Royale houses eateries and shops.

LOCATION: Epcot area
BIG DRAWS: Excellent value. Cheery environs with a decidedly Caribbean feel. Kids love the pirate-themed pool and select pirate-themed guestrooms.

Grand Floridian Resort & Spa

A romantic slice of Victorian confectionery, this resort recalls the opulent hotels that beckoned high society at the turn of the 20th century. The Grand Floridian's central building and five guest buildings—white structures laced with verandahs and turrets and topped with gabled roofs of red shingle—sprawl over acres of lakeside shorefront. Every glance embraces towering palms, stunning lake views, and rose gardens.

The impressive lobby features immense chandeliers, stained-glass skylights, and live piano and orchestra music. The resort also offers some of the best restaurants on Disney property.

LOCATION: Magic Kingdom area
BIG DRAWS: The height of luxury with a view of the Magic Kingdom. And it's just one monorail stop away from the World's original park.

225

Polynesian

This resort echoes the romance and beauty of the South Pacific with enchanting realism. Polynesian music is piped throughout the lushly landscaped grounds, which boast white-sand beaches, torches that burn nightly, and sufficient flowers to perfume the air.

Guest buildings, which are set amid tropical gardens, are named for Pacific islands. But the resort's centerpiece is unquestionably the Great Ceremonial house, which contains a three-story garden that all but consumes the atrium lobby.

LOCATION: Magic Kingdom area
BIG DRAWS: A breathtaking, you-are-there South Seas ambience makes the "Poly" exceptionally romantic. It's connected to the Magic Kingdom via monorail and water taxi. And the volcano pool is a huge kid-pleaser.

Port Orleans French Quarter

New Orleans's historic French Quarter is evoked in this resort's prim row-house-style buildings, which are wrapped in ornate wrought-iron railings and set amid romantic gardens and tree-lined blocks. Rooms are located in three-story buildings. The enclave is set alongside a stand-in Mississippi River, known as the Sassagoula.

LOCATION: Downtown Disney area (near Epcot)
BIG DRAWS: A good bang for the buck. It's the least sprawling of the moderate resorts. And kids get a big kick out of the pool area and sea serpent slide.

Port Orleans Riverside

Southern hospitality takes two forms at this resort: pillared mansions with groomed lawns, and upriver, rustic homes with tin roofs and bayou charm. The Sassagoula River curls around the resort's main recreation area like a moat. Bridges link guest lodgings with this area and the steamship-style building that houses the resort's eateries.

LOCATION: Downtown Disney area (near Epcot)
BIG DRAWS: Exceptional value. A lovely setting. "Royal" rooms are an option.

Saratoga Springs Resort & Spa

Long for the relaxation of a lakeside retreat—complete with fragrant gardens, bubbling fountains, and a spectacular spa? Look no further. This resort has all of the above, plus colorful Victorian architecture, rolling hills, and even a classic boardwalk. The property aims to recapture the charm and rejuvenating ambience of Saratoga Springs, New York, circa the late 1800s.

LOCATION: Downtown Disney area (near the Marketplace)
BIG DRAWS: A soothing spa and lovely pool area (zero-depth entry). A 10-minute stroll to the Downtown Disney entertainment district, this resort is a Disney Vacation Club property (but available to everyone).

Walt Disney World Resort Options

The following is a comprehensive list of Walt Disney World-owned-and-operated resort hotels. The information was correct at press time but is subject to change. In addition to Walt Disney World, it's possible to book vacations that pair a cruise with a hotel stay in Barcelona, Miami, Vancouver, or other destinations. For additional information, visit *www.disneycruise.com*, or call 800-951-3532.

DELUXE:
Animal Kingdom Lodge
BoardWalk
Contemporary Resort
Grand Floridian Resort & Spa
Old Key West
Polynesian Resort
Saratoga Springs Resort & Spa
Wilderness Lodge
Yacht & Beach Club

MODERATE:
Caribbean Beach Resort
Coronado Springs Resort
Port Orleans French Quarter
Port Orleans Riverside

VALUE:
All-Star Movies
All-Star Music
All-Star Sports
Art of Animation
Pop Century

Walt Disney World

Whether you plan to spend three days or three weeks, chances are you'll have a tough time taking in all of Walt Disney World. The vast resort boasts four theme parks, two water parks, full-service spas, championship golf, boating, waterskiing, tennis, fishing, parasailing, horseback riding, stock-car driving, and much more.

If your time is limited to a few days, we recommend visiting the theme parks and taking in the best attractions they have to offer (see pages 232–233). If you have the luxury of time, we suggest you stagger your visits to the parks, and intersperse peaceful respites by the pool, sporting activities, and shopping sprees. In any case, you'll also want to treat your-self to a classic Disney dining experience, even if it's simply an ice cream bar in the shape of you-know-who's head.

Theme Park Tickets

The process of selecting a ticket to Walt Disney World theme parks can leave your head spinning more than a whirl in a teacup. To simplify the process, ask yourself a few questions: How many days will I spend in the parks? Do I have a favorite park? Will I be making another trip to WDW this year? If you've got one day only, you should buy a one-day "Magic Your Way" base ticket. That will allow you to visit one theme park for one day. Easy, right? Now, if you're going to be spending two or more days in the theme parks, it gets a bit trickier. You can purchase a multi-day (from 2 to 10 days) base ticket and customize it. Would you like to park hop? That is, to visit more than one theme park on one day? You should purchase the park-hopping option. Do you plan to visit a water park during your stay?

HOT TIP

Many multi-day tickets can be purchased by phone or via the Internet; call 407-824-4321, or visit *www.disneyworld.com*. There is a $3 handling fee, but it's convenient to arrive with tickets in hand. Allow at least three weeks for delivery.

Perhaps a trip to the ESPN Wide World of Sports complex, WDW's Oak Trail golf course, and/or DisneyQuest (Downtown Disney arcade)? Consider adding the "Water Park Fun & More" option to your base ticket. Finally, if you might not have a chance to use all of the theme park days allotted by the ticket, ask for the "no expiration" option. This is a kind of insurance. It allows for a little more spontaneity during your trip, since you won't be obligated to use up your entire ticket. That said, if you don't spring for the "no expiration" option, *any unused days on the ticket will expire 14 days after it is first used.* No exceptions.

And last, there's the subject of an Annual Pass. What's that? You don't live in Florida, so how on Earth could this be worthwhile? The truth is, a premium annual pass costs about the same as a 10-day Magic Your Way ticket with all of the available bells and whistles. And, like the latter, it also includes admission to the water parks and Disney-Quest—plus a year of theme park admission. Annual passes net the bearer many discounts, including reduced resort rates.

Customized land and sea vacation packages may include 1- to 5-day Magic Your Way Tickets with Park Hopper Option. (Guests who customize their vacations themselves should customize their tickets accordingly.)

WDW RESTAURANT ROUNDUP

Walt's world is full of family-friendly dining establishments. Taking into consideration theming, value, and overall quality, these are some of our top table-service choices:

- Biergarten (Epcot)
- Boma—Flavors of Africa (Animal Kingdom Lodge)
- Cape May Cafe* (Beach Club resort)
- Chef Mickey's* (Contemporary resort)
- Cinderella's Royal Table* (Magic Kingdom)
- 50's Prime Time Cafe (Disney's Hollywood Studios)
- Garden Grill* (Epcot)
- Rainforest Cafe (Animal Kingdom and Downtown Disney)
- T-Rex: A Prehistoric Family Adventure (Downtown Disney Marketplace)
- Via Napoli (Epcot)
- The Wave . . . of American Flavors (Contemporary resort)

* Disney characters are in attendance for at least one of the meals offered by the eatery.

HOT TIP

To book a table at a WDW restaurant, call 407-WDW-DINE (939-3463) up to 180 days ahead. Call to confirm it before you leave home!

A Whirlwind World Tour

No matter how long you plan to stay at Walt Disney World, deciding what to do first can be a challenge. When it comes to the theme parks, if we had four days, we'd visit them in this order: Magic Kingdom, Epcot, Disney's Hollywood Studios, and Animal Kingdom. Since the Magic Kingdom is our favorite (and tops with most kids), we'd be sure to hop back to it once or twice. When it comes to narrowing the list of theme park "must-sees" to the barely manageable, we recommend the following attractions and shows that we believe stand head, shoulders, and ears above the rest.

Magic Kingdom*

- Splash Mountain
- Space Mountain
- Big Thunder Mountain Railroad
- Pirates of the Caribbean
- The Haunted Mansion
- Peter Pan's Flight
- Mickey's PhilharMagic
- Buzz Lightyear's Space Ranger Spin
- It's a Small World
- The Seven Dwarfs Mine Train
- The Many Adventures of Winnie the Pooh
- Wishes (fireworks show)

* With young children: Dumbo the Flying Elephant, The Many Adventures of Winnie the Pooh, Under the Sea—Journey of the Little Mermaid, It's a Small World, Cinderella's Golden Carrousel, Tomorrowland Speedway, Walt Disney World Railroad, Enchanted Tales with Belle, and The Country Bear Jamboree.

Epcot*

- Soarin' (Living with the Land pavilion)
- Spaceship Earth
- Test Track
- Turtle Talk with Crush (The Seas pavilion)
- Mission: SPACE (the less-intense, non-spinning version)
- IllumiNations: Reflections of Earth (fireworks show)
- The American Adventure
- Ellen's Energy Adventure (Universe of Energy pavilion)

* With young children: The Seas with Nemo & Friends, ImageWorks play area in the Imagination! pavilion, Mexico's boat ride, and Kidcot Funstops in World Showcase.

Disney's Hollywood Studios*

- Toy Story Mania!
- The Twilight Zone™ Tower of Terror
- Rock 'n' Roller Coaster
- Beauty and the Beast— Live on Stage
- Muppet*Vision 3-D
- Star Tours—the Adventures Continue
- The Great Movie Ride
- Fantasmic! (a combination fireworks/stage show)

* With young children: Voyage of The Little Mermaid, Muppet*Vision 3-D, Honey, I Shrunk the Kids Movie Set Adventure, Disney Junior—Live on Stage!, and Beauty and the Beast—Live on Stage.

HOT TIP

As the definitive source of insider information, we highly (and immodestly) recommend *Birnbaum's Official Guide to Walt Disney World 2014.*

Animal Kingdom*

- Expedition Everest
- Dinosaur
- Kali River Rapids
- Kilimanjaro Safaris
- It's Tough to be a Bug!
- Festival of the Lion King
- Pangani Forest Exploration Trail
- Maharajah Jungle Trek
- Finding Nemo—the Musical
- Flights of Wonder

* With young children: The Oasis, Festival of the Lion King, DinoLand, The Boneyard playground, Maharajah Jungle Trek, Pangani Forest Exploration Trail, and the Kilimanjaro Safaris.

INDEX